# Trading on Target

Founded in 1807, John Wiley & Sons is the oldest independent publishing company in the United States. With offices in North America, Europe, Australia, and Asia, Wiley is globally committed to developing and marketing print and electronic products and services for our customers' professional and personal knowledge and understanding.

The Wiley Trading series features books by traders who have survived the market's ever-changing temperament and have prospered—some by reinventing systems, others by getting back to basics. Whether a novice trader, professional, or somewhere in-between, these books will provide the advice and strategies needed to prosper today and well into the future.

For a list of available titles, visit our web site at www.WileyFinance.com.

# Trading on Target

## *How to Cultivate a Winner's State of Mind*

**ADRIENNE TOGHRAIE**

WILEY

John Wiley & Sons, Inc.

*Bodhi and Gingko*



Published by John Wiley & Sons, Inc., Hoboken, New Jersey.
Published simultaneously in Canada.



For general information on our other products and services or for technical support, please contact our Customer Care Department within the United States at (800) 762-2974, outside the United States at (317) 572-3993, or fax (317) 572-4002.

Wiley also publishes its books in a variety of electronic formats. Some content that appears in print may not be available in electronic books. For more information about Wiley products, visit our web site at www.wiley.com.

***Library of Congress Cataloging-in-Publication Data:***

Toghraie, Adrienne Laris.
Trading on target : how to cultivate a winners state of mind / Adrienne Toghraie.
p. cm. – (Wiley trading series)
Includes index.
ISBN 978-1-118-06491-7 (hardback); ISBN 978-1-118-08677-3 (ebk);
ISBN 978-1-118-08678-0 (ebk); ISBN 978-1-118-08679-7 (ebk)
1. Investment analysis. 2. Investments. 3. Success in business. I. Title.
HG4529.T594 2011
332.64–dc22 2011005438

Printed in the United States of America

10 9 8 7 6 5 4 3 2 1

# Contents

# Foreword

Adrienne has done it again! In her latest published volume, *Trading on Target*, she presents a down-to-earth, easy-to-read common sense book for the practical trader in any market. Learn about the real-life facets of trading discipline, as Adrienne takes your hand and leads you through the sometimes tricky mechanics of self-discipline and self-control.

There are few authors in the area of help for traders who write with Adrienne's clarity. The interesting thing is that when you read her books you wonder: "how does she know I'm having these problems?" Those thoughts and feelings that you've been vaguely aware of are now brought into focus as if a fog has been lifted. You can now define and hopefully anticipate the way you will react to price action.

Adrienne and I have been friends for some time. We have collaborated at seminars and webinars so I know of her dedication to traders everywhere. The answers to the "whats" and "whys" of market discipline are explained in plain, precise language which should be easily understood by old-timers and new traders alike.

This book gives you the nuts and bolts of what you need to become a psychologically and emotionally mature trader. The lessons are taken from the lives of real traders, traders who have struggled through the very things that may be holding you back.

Adrienne pulls it all together: the attitudes, perceptions, and insights you will need to reach the heights of trading success. She will also give you solutions to handle the oldest psychological and emotional hang-ups commonly found among those who aspire to succeed in trading.

In reviewing my past 53 years of trading, I found Adrienne's *Trading on Target* a refreshing, informative, and rewarding work.

Joe Ross<br>
Trader, Author, Speaker, Mentor<br>
*Trading Educators*

# Preface

It always surprises me that, after 21 years in the business of working on trader discipline, I would have more to write about. But traders never fail me with the material they offer. Even if some of the information has been said before in another way, very often this new approach will be beneficial for a new understanding.

On a larger note, wherever you are in your ability as a trader, there is always room to grow. There is an old adage "When the student is ready, the teacher arrives." What I have found to be true is that, "When the student is ready, he will hear the words from a teacher in a way that he has never heard them before." There have been many times when a client will write to me and say, "My trading improved dramatically after we worked together, but that article you just wrote took it to a new level."

*Trading On Target* is about overcoming the self-imposed limitations that keep traders from the next level of success. With each trader who I have worked with privately, I have grown in my skills as a trader's success coach. These skills have led to new insights, which are the basis of this book.

The way traders approach the markets has changed over the years because of new technology. Also, traders are now more inclined to accept the psychology of trading without feeling threatened. For this reason, in this book I can be more straightforward in how I present this material.

One of the main differences in the way traders think about the psychology of trading, from when I first started my business, is that traders are more inclined to want to seek out whatever it takes to improve themselves psychologically. They feel comfortable talking about their issues to their peers as well as to me.

Traders have told me that reading about the real life experiences of other traders who have overcome their issues, makes them feel like they can face their own. Having specific exercises—that are included in this book—gives traders a vehicle for starting to improve their performances. It also makes traders aware of those areas where they need help.

I have enjoyed the journey of assisting many traders to reach high levels of success and will continue to do so. Welcome aboard.

# Acknowledgments

A special thanks to all of the traders who contributed their stories so that everyone could learn from their lessons.

Another special thanks to the following magazines, newsletters, and web sites that have published articles and interviews: *SFO Magazine*, *Tech Talk with Don Vialoux*, *Technical Analysis of Stocks and Commodities Magazine*, *Traders World Magazine*, *Trading on Target Newsletter*, and *Your Trading Edge Magazine*.

# About the Author

**Adrienne Toghraie,** Trader's Success Coach, is an internationally recognized authority in the field of human development and a master practitioner of Neuro-Linguistic Programming (NLP) for the financial and business communities. She is the founder and president of *Trading on Target* and *Enriching Life Seminars*, two companies dedicated to helping traders, sales people, and other high achievers to dramatically increase profits and success in all areas of life. Using her 21 years of study in the science of Modeling Excellence/NLP and numerous other forms of psychological development, Toghraie has helped her clients to push through their self-imposed limitations to extraordinary and documented new levels of success.

Adrienne's articles and interviews have been featured in most of the major financial trade magazines and newspapers throughout the world. She has authored *Get A life: Treasure Diary for Creating Wealth and Happiness*, *The Winning Edge 2: Traders' and Investors' Psychological Coach in a Book*, *The Winning Edge 3: Traders' and Investors' Coaching to Excellence*, *The Winning Edge 4: Traders' and Investors' Greater Success*, *Traders' Secrets* co-authored with Murray Ruggiero and *The Winning Edge, How to Use Your Personal Psychological Power in Trading and Investing* with Jake Bernstein.

Adrienne's public seminars and private counseling, as well as her television appearances and keynote addresses at major industry conferences, have achieved a wide level of recognition and popularity.

PART I

# Obstacles to Becoming a Top Trader

*Your success will reflect the history of your life, unless you transform how you interpret the stories of your past.*

CHAPTER 1

# Mirror, Mirror

Take a good look into the mirror of your life. What do you see? If you are willing to look deeply, you will find the obstacle to achieving greater success. This obstacle is You. While you spend your time crunching out indicators and plotting out money management, you also need to look into the other choices you make in your daily life, because those choices affect how you make trading decisions.

Here are some of the choices you make that most clearly reflect the problems in your trading.

## CHOOSING HOW YOU LIVE: YOUR ENVIRONMENT

Trading problems are often reflected in the environment in which you choose to live. If your physical environment is a mess, chances are that your trading is a mess, too. And so it was with John, one of my clients.

John's parents learned to be clever out of necessity. They were poor immigrants from Yugoslavia who escaped Communism with nothing more than the clothes on their backs and the determination to create a safe life for themselves in America. They educated themselves, grew their own business, and established a foundation of wealth. John remembers growing up in a home that was full of things that other people would have discarded. And so it became John's habit as well never to throw away anything, because it could be useful some day. He was living with his parents' mindset even though his inheritance left him with more than a million dollars in the bank, a mortgage-free home, and a monthly trust fund stipend that provided enough for an average lifestyle for the rest of his life.

John became a trader after becoming bored with his chosen field of engineering. He set out to do whatever it took to be profitable without taking risk. Anyone who knew trading would be impressed with his mathematical equations and indicators, but he was stuck at the gate. Every time he would try paper trading to prove his system, he would find it necessary to tweak it. What John was doing was trying to create a situation where he would not have to take any risk. When I asked John to start throwing away anything that he thought he would never use again, he found it impossible. In frustration he asked me an all-too-familiar question, "What does this have to do with trading and making money?" I told John that until he was willing to let go of the beliefs of his parents, he would never have the mindset of taking the risk necessary to be a successful trader.

### Solution: Reflect Order

If you look into the mirror of your life and you see physical disorder, you need to address the problem. Unfortunately, when disorder and chaos take over your living space, you cannot simply wave a magic wand and make it all disappear. However, the good news is that over time, the problem can be completely corrected. I have helped traders bring order back into their lives through the following process:

- The first step is to decide on one very small area that could be cleaned and organized in a matter of a few minutes at most. Then, do it! Make it something so painless that it cannot create any fear or discomfort.
- As soon as you have accomplished this first step, praise yourself.
- Repeat these steps.
- As you begin to see progress, you can take on projects that are a little larger, but never set yourself major goals as this will cause you to feel overwhelmed.

Remember, that no one can eat a 10-tier chocolate cake in one large mouthful. But, anyone can do it a spoonful at a time.

## CHOOSING HOW YOU TAKE CARE OF YOUR OUTER SELF: YOUR DRESS AND APPEARANCE

Dress appropriately to feel good about yourself, because you will respond emotionally to your own appearance the same way you respond emotionally to other people's choices about their appearances.

So, what do you see in the mirror today? If you see yourself sitting at the computer unshaven, in pajamas, and barefoot, your appearance may be reflecting the source of your trading problems. One of the lessons I have learned from attending countless trade shows is that I can spot a highly successful trader from a hundred feet away. He is rarely the sloppy fellow with the five o'clock shadow who looks like he needs a shower. He will have a clean-cut appearance with an air of confidence about him.

### Solution: Reflect a Well-Dressed Image

Just as the state of your physical environment may reflect disorder in your trading, your physical appearance may do so, too. Taking care of your appearance tells your unconscious mind that you are in control of your world and that you care about yourself, as well as promoting discipline in your life. When you look in the mirror and see a person proud of his appearance, your unconscious reflects that success. All of these messages provide positive instructions for your unconscious mind.

Part of looking good is looking healthy and fit. So, wearing even the most expensive clothes will not obscure the fact that you make unhealthy choices in your diet and exercise regimen. If you bulge in the middle, and if your skin and hair look unhealthy, you will not be able to hide it from your mirror.

## CHOOSING HOW YOU TAKE CARE OF YOUR INNER SELF: YOUR THOUGHTS AND EMOTIONS

When you look carefully at your face in the mirror, you will see your own thoughts and feelings reflected in your eyes and in the corners of your mouth. Is it a happy, determined, positive, content, or successful aura that you see? Is it a depressed, bitter, frightened, or resigned face that looks back at you? If we can read those powerful emotions in the faces of those around us, we can learn to see them in ourselves, as well. So take a good long look.

Our thoughts determine our emotions, which in turn determine our behaviors. If our thoughts are negative, pessimistic, self-deprecating, and finger pointing, our emotions will be dark, full of depression and anger, and energy depleting. Our trading will reflect those thoughts and emotions. With such powerful inner forces at work, it is easy to see how a trader would have difficulty dealing with the inevitable losses that are a natural part of trading.

A trader named Phil had been struggling with his trading for many years, unable to rise above mediocre results. It was obvious, however, after our first session together that the problem was clearly reflected in the choices he made in his thoughts. Phil was quick to talk about the negative, and eager to look for ways to prove that he was wronged by the markets and by everyone around him. When Phil looked in the mirror, all he saw was a victim. His poor performance was a perfect reflection of his self-defeating self-talk. What Phil needed to do was to actually listen to his own self-talk to see how he sabotaged his own success.

### Solution: Choose Positive, Life-Affirming, Motivating Self-Talk

You may not be able to see your words in a mirror, but you can certainly see their effects on your face. How can you stop choosing negative, sabotaging self-talk?

- The first step is to start noticing how you talk to yourself when you are not following your rules in trading. Do not try to censor your thoughts. Just observe them. What are you really telling yourself? It helps to write down what you are saying to yourself to discover what is really going on in your mind. Remember, your words will affect your emotions, and your emotions will affect your performance. So, listen carefully.
- Once you have spent some time observing and listening to your own self talk, it is time to correct it. When you hear yourself saying something negative, correct it with a positive statement. For example, if you hear yourself saying, "There I go again, doing something stupid," correct yourself with a statement such as, "I learn useful lessons from my mistakes."
- Each time you say something positive, praise yourself by saying, "good catch" to anchor in the new behavior.
- Continue listening to your self-talk and to the self-talk of others, and it will make you even more aware of negative talk. This will eventually cause you to translate your negative self-talk into positive statement anchors.

## CHOOSING HOW YOU TAKE CARE OF YOUR INNER SELF: YOUR SPIRITUAL LIFE

Once again, looking deeply into the mirror, you can see reflected there the peace or lack of it that comes from having cultivated a spiritual life or not having done so. Traders who become obsessed with the bottom line and forget about the top line can lose the inner peace that is essential to a long and happy trading career. For example, Keith was a trader who was so obsessed with his trading that he failed to develop the other parts of his life. When his wife died from breast cancer, his entire world collapsed, along with his trading. He had no inner resources from which to draw, and he had no spiritual life to help him deal with this enormous loss in his life.

### Solution: Find a Spiritual Practice That Brings You Inner Peace

Because there is no one spiritual practice that is right for everyone, you may need to look around for the one that fits your needs and values. You may decide that the religious tradition of your childhood is the one that feels best, or you may find that you have outgrown it. In any case, prayer and/or meditative practices are powerful means to bring you peace. Once you have begun to achieve that inner peace, it will show in your face and be reflected in your trading.

## CHOOSING HOW YOU INTERACT WITH THE OUTSIDE WORLD: YOUR RELATIONSHIPS AND YOUR CONTRIBUTIONS TO THE COMMUNITY

When you look into the mirror, you can also see the faces of the people standing next to you. Who are they and what do their faces tell you? Do you see a happy and loving family and a large circle of friends surrounding you? Do you see a community of people around you who are grateful for the contributions that you make to them? Or do you stand alone, without a loving support system? In either case, your trading reflects what you see. A trader with a strong support system can face losses and problems in his trading. He knows that there are strong relationships from which he can draw support, understanding, and sympathy. He knows why he gets up in the morning and what his trading means to his life in a way that gives him motivation to succeed. A trader who contributes to the community feels good about himself and in turn, receives respect and appreciation. All of these positive forces contribute to the look of confidence, self-esteem, and security in his face. But, what happens if a trader has chosen unwisely in his personal life and has surrounded himself with toxic relationships or none at all?

### Solution 1: First Develop a Good Relationship with Yourself, and Then Reach out to Others from Strength and Caring

A trader who has troubled relationships with others often has a troubled relationship with himself, which, in turn, usually results from a troubled relationship with his past. Healing wounds from the past is a major undertaking. Relationship issues, then, are just the symptom of deeper problems. There may also be addiction issues, and/or destructive attitudes and patterns of behavior to correct before a trader can move forward with good relationships. When deep, unresolved issues are the barriers to good relationships, much of the work needed to correct these problems should be done with the assistance or guidance of trained professionals. Otherwise, the bandages used to patch up the wounds will easily come unglued.

### Solution 2: Get Involved and Get Out of the House

If the problem is not a deep one but simply a result of too much time spent trading and not enough living, then the time has come to find a way to get involved. Each community has a wealth of civic and social organizations, churches, clubs, adult education programs, charities, and activities of every kind. Something in all that mix will provide an isolated trader with an opening into the world of social interaction and friendships. The only requirement is that he must get out of his own small world and temporarily close the door behind him.

## CONCLUSION

As difficult as it is to take a hard look in the mirror, the answers to many of your trading problems are right there for you to see. Each day we make choices about how we will take care of ourselves, our environment, and our relationships. If we consistently choose wisely, the results will shine forth in the mirror, and will be reflected in our trading. We will see the same confidence, energy, and success in our trading that we see in our faces. If we fail to make good and healthy choices, eventually we will see the same anemic and negative forces in our faces that we see in our trading. The choice is ours and the mirror does not lie.

---

*Perfectionism creates stress, but working toward the best possible outcome allows you to have the best outcome possible.*

---

CHAPTER 2

# The Perfection Trap

Are you the perfect trader? Do you want to be? Do you seek the perfect trade, the one that unlocks all the doors to your dreams? Are you trying to create the perfect trading system? If so, you may also be unwilling to settle for anything less than the perfect house, perfect car, perfect spouse, perfect schools for your children, perfect vacation, and the perfect night's sleep to refresh you perfectly for the perfect day to come?

If you could achieve all of that perfection in your life, would it make you happy? Content? A better trader? A better spouse and parent? A better human being?

## MR. PERFECTION

Roy is a brilliant man with an enormous capacity to achieve success as a professional trader and in his personal life. The problem is that he actually achieves and produces very little because he is obsessed with doing everything perfectly and in having everything perfect. For that reason, Roy has spent much of the past 25 years working on creating the perfect trading system. Periodically, he allows himself to feel that his system is ready to trade and once again he trades in real time. At first, his system will perform . . . you guessed it . . . perfectly and he will make a killing in the market for at least a month and possibly more. At this point, he will call me and wax poetic about the perfection of his system. But shortly thereafter, his system will begin to generate some losses as well, and as soon as that happens, Roy's trading goes into a steep decline. Within a brief time, he will have given back everything he made in the markets and sometimes a bit more.

Once this cycle ends, Roy will begin all over again to fiddle with his system until it is perfect and will create only profits and no losses.

And what about Roy's perfect life? Well, Roy is not married because he has never found the perfect woman. He has had many girlfriends, but he falls out of love with each one as soon as he discovers her imperfections. He does not own a house because he could never settle on one—there was always a problem with each home in which he has lived. In fact, he has moved literally dozens of times throughout the course of his adulthood. When Roy begins a project, he works on it compulsively, attempting to make it perfect, which is impossible. So, he fiddles with it endlessly, unable to let it go. The list of his life's incompletions continues to grow longer and longer.

## PERFECTION AND SUCCESS

Achieving success in any endeavor is difficult enough without adding the complication of trying to achieve perfection at the same time. Anyone who has ever used a Microsoft product knows that perfection was never achieved, never even close. But Microsoft cornered the market. It got its customers close enough. And yes, it did so in a sloppy and non-intuitive way. But, it entered the market in a timely fashion. Had it waited to achieve perfection, it would have entered the race too late to win.

In trading, there is no perfection to be achieved. There is no perfect trading system, there are no perfect trades, and there is no perfect trader. Losses are a natural part of the process—in fact, you could almost say that losses are a perfect part of a trading system. The object is to limit the losses so that your gains outpace your losses. The object should never be to completely eliminate any chance of losses. This would mean that you had fallen into the Perfection Trap.

## HOW IT ALL BEGINS

Roy's own confinement in the perfection trap happened so young that he never had a chance to escape. His parents were critical and demanding from the day that Roy gained consciousness. Roy could never please them. Regardless of how hard he tried to be perfect, his parents would always find something with which to find fault. To make matters worse, they also withheld praise and approval. The result was that Roy learned at the most critical point in the development of his worldview that the most important thing in life was to achieve perfection.

Here are six of the major paths by which traders arrive in the perfection trap:

1. Perfection-demanding parents

   This, of course, is Roy's background. But it is a common one. The faces may be different, but the result is the same. Parents are fearful of their own inadequacy at not being perfect. Since they were probably raised in an equally critical and approval-withholding environment, they do not see the harm they are doing in repeating the pattern on their innocent children.

2. Fear of failure and loss

   Some traders arrive at the point of demanding perfection in their trading after experiencing the pain of loss. Rather than dealing with those feelings and working their way through them, they foreswear ever experiencing that kind of pain again. But, the only way to never again experience a trading loss is to become the perfect trader. Each time the trader experiences another loss he is even more determined to be less vulnerable by being more perfect.

3. Praise for being perfect

   The reverse of the highly critical family life is the one in which the child is praised over and over again for achieving perfection—in school with perfect grades, in sports and performance situations, in solving problems, or achieving goals. This praise and recognition can come from parents, but it can also come from teachers, coaches, other family members and friends, and even from total strangers. The physiological rush that comes from that kind of praise can imprint on a vulnerable young mind the desire to experience the rush again and again. It is exactly like the reaction the brain has to an addictive drug.

4. Perfection-obsessed cultural forces

   If you watch television commercials, you will hear the word "perfect" used more and more frequently: perfect weddings, perfect vacation, perfect home, perfect lawn, perfect sunset. In fact, the word perfect is nearly ubiquitous in the advertising barrage of our senses. Spend a day home sick lying on your sofa watching commercial television and start counting the times that the word perfect comes up in the ads, not to mention the programming itself. Of course, it is not just television but all the media that are infected with this notion of perfection. The notion of perfection being the endgame for all human endeavors has taken on a value beyond its usefulness. But the result is a subconscious infection in the minds of far too many.

5. Feelings of insecurity and loss of value

   When a trader has deep-seated feelings of inadequacy, insecurity, and/or worthlessness, he will often attempt to overcompensate by attempting to achieve perfection in his work and in his environment. Achieving perfection will prove his worth and settle any doubts he or others may have about him. Of course, the harder he strives for perfection, the more insecure he actually appears to the outside world.
6. The fear of loss of control

   In a profession in which a trader can easily feel that he has little or no control, the achievement of perfection can quell any sense of not being in control. For the insecure, achieving perfection means that you have total control.

What all of these factors have in common, at their very base, is fear. The achievement of perfection makes an individual feel all-powerful. In fact, the achievement of perfection is as close to godliness as we can come. But the piper must be paid, as we will see . . .

## FOR TRADERS: THE COST OF PURSUING PERFECTION

Just as the Pied Piper demanded his payment, it is easy to see what four of the not-so-hidden costs of the pursuit of perfection might be by looking at Roy's experience, as well as those of other traders who are stuck in the Perfection Trap:

1. Difficulty in taking action

   To demand perfect trades that do not generate losses means that a trader will hesitate each and every time he should be taking action based on the signals he gets from his system/methodology. Instead of perfect trades, this hesitation can lead to no trades or bad trades. The demands of perfection can progress from hesitation, to difficulty in taking action, to inability to take action, which means that trading stops altogether.
2. Loss of self-discipline

   Instead of increasing self-discipline, the pursuit of perfection will ultimately undermine self-discipline by putting unreasonable pressure on the individual trader to be perfect. At first, the pursuit of perfection may guide a trader to a more and more disciplined practice. But as time passes, he will feel obliged to raise the bar higher and higher. In Roy's experience, this usually resulted in a total collapse of his discipline, like a dieter who succumbs to bingeing after a diet that is too rigid. For a trader, this means the sudden abandonment of the controls on his trading, which can lead to significant losses.

3. Instability

   Like Roy who moved from place to place looking for the perfect environment for his trading and his living space, a trader seeking perfection will find that he is constantly uprooting his life. Whether he is perpetually on the move, remodeling, or changing spouses or partners, this trader's life will be riddled with instability. Unfortunately for him, one of the most important cornerstones of a successful trader's life is stability.

4. Unhappy, unfulfilled personal life

   The pursuit of perfection in trading will almost surely spill over into a trader's personal life. The search for the perfect spouse will result in divorce, one after another. It will also result in the alienation of one's children and friendships. A trader who feels that he has found the "perfect mate" will make his new love feel as though she is a queen. He will shower her with praise and presents, setting her up on a pedestal. But, she will be in for a rude awakening after he discovers that she is not a goddess, but only a human being. If stability is essential to a trader's success, a happy and supportive home life is the basis of that stability.

## GETTING OUT OF THE TRAP AND BACK ONTO THE GREEN

Although the allure of perfection is a very powerful one, as we have seen, it is possible to loosen its grip on a trader's life. There are four steps to getting out of the perfection trap:

1. The first step in escaping the perfection trap, of course, is the recognition that you are in its possession. As you read this article, did you see yourself in it? Do you recognize your own need to be perfect, to have the "perfect things" in your life?
2. If you feel that you have a problem with perfection, take an honest assessment of your own perfection trap:
   - How long have you been in it?
   - What makes you feel that you need to have perfection in your life (where did it come from)?
   - How do you apply it to yourself? To your trading? To the significant others in your life?

- How does it affect your trading? What would change in your trading if you stopped trying to be perfect and just focused on following your trading methodology?
- What are you getting from trying to be perfect—what is the payoff for you? Is it a sense of being in control? Of being more worthy of love and admiration? Of reducing fear of loss and pain?

3. Once you have looked at the underlying causes and the nature of your own perfection trap, write a list of the things in your life that it has cost you. What have you given up? For example:
   - Peace of mind
   - Tolerance and/or unconditional love of the people closest to you
   - Friends, family, and children
   - Enjoyment of the process of trading
   - Professional success
4. Now imagine what it would be like to give up the notion that you must achieve perfection. What would you gain? To answer that question, you can simply look at the list you wrote for step three. At this point, you must decide if the benefits of endlessly seeking perfection outweigh the cost and the potential gain of not trying to be perfect.

## THE ALTERNATIVE

So, you are asking, if I give up my quest for perfection, what will I have in its place? Will the result be chaos, mediocrity, poverty, sloth, and crudeness all around me? Of course not! You can still exercise good taste and high standards. But you can allow yourself to be satisfied with a job well done or done to the best you can do. You will discover that very good and excellent can also bring you outstanding results. And now you can sit back and take pleasure in the foibles and shortcomings in others as they display their desire for "perfection." You can relax and enjoy the process of trading. And best of all, you can learn to appreciate all that you have. The result will be that you can now trade with a sense of joy, with the knowledge that loss is coming and it is okay because it is built into your system, that you are supported by family and friends, and that each day is a gift. Oh, and by the way, your trading will almost certainly advance to the next step.

---

*If you do not allow for silent moments in your life, looping stories of self-talk will interfere with you accomplishing you goals.*

---

CHAPTER 3

# Deep Freeze

At a recent professional basketball game, an eighth grade girl was preparing to experience the thrill of a lifetime. She had been selected to sing "The Star Spangled Banner" before a large and enthusiastic audience. Instead of experiencing the thrill of success, she forgot the words to the song and froze. The humiliation and embarrassment that swept over her added to the whirlwind of fear that consumed her. At that moment, the coach for the Portland Trail Blazers, Maurice Cheeks, appeared at her side and started to sing while encouraging her to follow. This kind and courageous man melted her freeze and she finished the song triumphantly.

Just as this young lady froze at the very moment she needed to be performing at her best, traders frequently find themselves freezing at the moment when they should be trading at their best. Instead of pulling the trigger to take that trade or exiting at the pre-determined stop, they freeze. The result is that they stand by and watch helplessly as a tremendous opportunity passes them by or their losses continue to pile up into a financial catastrophe. Afterward, filled with remorse, guilt, and self-recrimination, they search for reasons and justifications for their failure.

## THE GREEN GIANT

Even the best traders can experience the Deep Freeze. In fact, the better a trader is and the longer he has been successful, the more likely it is that he will face a Deep Freeze experience on occasion. Top professionals in all fields of endeavor experience this phenomenon. An example would be Tiger Woods in a PGA Masters' Tournament at Augusta, Georgia. He had his eye on his third Green Jacket. If he had won, it would have made him the only golfer to ever win the PGA Masters' three times in a row, claiming the symbol of being the best. But even one of the most focused athletes in the world can experience deep freeze moments when thrown psychologically off course.

How could this happen to such a consummate professional who is so accustomed to winning and handling stress? This set of expectations is exactly what can undermine the concentration of a winner. When a professional is accustomed to winning, he can be completely thrown off his game when something unexpected happens that puts him at a disadvantage. This is what happened to Tiger. A slight misstep, a tiny loss of concentration that created an unexpected deviation in the layout of a shot resulted in him being less than Tiger. Since the failure to perform at his peak was no longer in Tiger's mental player's book, suddenly, he was off his game and off the mark for the third Green Jacket.

Once a professional trader finds himself off his game after a deep freeze experience, he may lose confidence. Unaccustomed to losing confidence, he will lose more confidence and become uncertain of his ability, fearful that he has lost the magic. He will become embarrassed that he is not winning, and ultimately, become less and less capable of recreating his personal miracles.

## DOING TRADER FREEZE

Recently, a trader named Don took my Trader's Evaluation. From his evaluation, his foundation for psychological stability appeared to be exceptional. He was highly disciplined in his professional and personal life. He consistently practiced healthy patterns of thought and behavior. His preparation for trading was impressive and he maintained continued professional and personal development. His childhood and current family life appeared to be healthy, functional, and supportive of his trading activities. His attitudes, beliefs, and emotional underpinnings were sound and bolstering for success. But the question remained: Why would he freeze at following his rules? The only way Don was going to change the pattern he had developed was for me to help him uncover the hidden root cause of the problem and help him to reprogram his associations and reactions.

## INSPECTRESS CLOUSSEAU, AT YOUR SERVICE

First, we had to discover how Don constructed his thinking. We needed this information to reprogram and reanchor the associations that were blocking his pathway to success. What were the beliefs, attitudes, values, decisions, and experiences that built the foundation of his perceptions and created the weakness that sabotaged his performance when he needed it the most? Everything he said about his background looked supportive of success in life. In fact, the success he experienced in his business life before choosing trading as a career confirmed the soundness of his qualifications.

Don had difficulty in completing one homework assignment. The task had been to recall unhappy life experiences. Except for losses in trading, Don could only recall one single life event that was not positive. He remembered a childhood experience where he was playing with matches and started a fire in a haystack next to the family barn. As the flames leapt toward the barn and the family home, he could see them being consumed by flames in his mind's eye. Rushing to his mother in a panic, he found that he could not speak. His mother shouted at him to focus, but he could only verbalize one word: "FIRE!"

Fortunately, his mother reacted quickly enough to avert a major disaster. The vision in Don's imagination of the barn going up in flames was enough to impress upon him the importance of making choices in life that would not result in dire consequences or major loss. The result of this experience was his determination to study each decision and make certain that he had eliminated as much risk as possible. He had certainly exercised caution and due diligence in his decision-making process of hiring me as a coach, checking out references, and quizzing me on each point.

Don had approached becoming a trader with the same caution he had displayed in his earlier life. He had back tested his results to give himself the confidence that his system would work. Then, he forward tested it by paper trading to make sure that he felt comfortable taking the signals. But as many traders find out, trading with real money is the final test of being able to trade. Don had trained his neurological system to put up a warning sign in the form of freezing, not taking action when his comfort level was being challenged. Although the words "Your decision could take down the barn" were not in his head, the feelings that resulted from the hay fire were deeply anchored in him and prevented him from being consistent in following his trading rules.

## OVERWHELMING YOUR NEURO-NETWORKING

A principal cause of emotional paralysis is the association we form with taking action under duress. Like Don, most traders have experienced situations in their youth when they were confronted with a crisis or a moment of great stress for which they were unprepared. If they were bewildered by powerful emotion, conflicting information, or a tremendous amount of sensory input from their environment, their likely reaction at that time was to freeze. They may have wanted to act but could not. Afterward, they replayed the experience over and over in their mind's eye, reliving the feelings of fear and uncertainty. Then, they added the feelings of shame and distress for not having acted. Powerful emotions such as fear and embarrassment burn the experience deeply into the human psyche, forever associating a situation that is unexpected and stressful with an inability to act.

Actually, the deep freeze reaction is a form of self-defense in nature. Many animals, when faced with no immediate opening for flight or fight, will freeze in their tracks. This is not a great strategy in the path of an oncoming car traveling at 65 miles per hour. But, it clearly can have an advantage in nature, giving the potential victim the time to assess the situation and garner strength for escape. Unfortunately, it can be a financially fatal strategy for traders who must make timely trading decisions that can either make or lose a great deal of money with each tick of the second hand.

## INTO THE MIND OF PERFORMANCE ANXIETY

Just as Tiger Woods could freeze when confronted with a situation for which he was unprepared, all performers, including traders, are capable of freezing when confronted with something unexpected. Performance is enhanced when the player trains through repetitive action. Recently, competitors have been training more and more with mental rehearsals in addition to the actual physical repetition. Mental rehearsal allows a competitor to try new and possibly dangerous actions in his mind before he ever attempts them in reality. The benefits of mental rehearsal are well documented by Olympic athletes from around the world.

Traders can also use mental rehearsal to test their trading techniques. When paper trading, a trader is using mental rehearsal to trade. He sees himself taking the trade even though there is no money at stake. Also, he has the opportunity to see how he would trade if his money were actually on the line. This type of practice is essential to successful trading since it preserves capital while a trader is learning the profession.

The problem with paper trading and mental rehearsal is that it does not address the fact that most people cannot disconnect themselves from the emotional value they give to real money. When real money is on the line, underlying issues rise to the surface with the power to freeze action. These issues are expressed in self-talk in the following examples:

- What about all of the hard work I invested to earn this money in the first place?

- It's not fair to risk my family's security.
- My spouse has been so supportive, what happens if I screw up?
- This is part of the family retirement fund, savings account, vacation money, and the children's education that I have on the line.
- If I am not able to make a living, I will have to get a real job.
- Money made from trading is easy money. I need to work hard or I don't deserve it.
- The markets change all the time. How do I know that this moment isn't one of them?

Does any of this self-talk sound familiar?

What follows from this self-talk is an intense feeling that can lead to the deep freeze.

## CHANGING THE DOMINO EFFECT

The root cause event creates a limiting belief or a conflict. This leads to an intense feeling, followed by nonaction or delayed action. So, the chain that leads to the paralyzing feeling must be broken. The most effective way to break the chain is to reprogram the root cause, which changes the belief or conflict. If the underlying cause is unknown or buried too deeply for the individual to access, this process becomes too difficult for the individual to accomplish without the help of a professional. However, the most effective way to proceed is to not allow the feelings to develop in the first place. This is accomplished by taking steps that prepare you to act rather than becoming frozen by limiting emotions.

Preparation is the antidote for emotional overload. When a United States military officer was asked about the performance of his young and untested Marines in the Iraqi War, he talked about an assault where they were unexpectedly under fire. The situation was overwhelming but instead of panicking, they reverted to their training and came through the attack admirably. Their training had been so complete that they were able to handle a situation that was unique, unexpected, and profoundly dangerous without going into the deep freeze. Plus, they did not have access to the resources that those in the comfort of their homes have to dispel their fear and panic. What they had was something far more potent than drugs or alcohol—they had preparation.

This is a mental rehearsal that can help you prepare for taking the trade rather than deep freezing:

- Mentally rehearse everything that could go wrong and right with the best possible outcome.

- Make sure in your mental rehearsal that you say positive words to yourself that make you feel good just before taking the trade. "I will get good results because I follow my plan."
- When you see the right set up, repeat your positive statement.
- Physically change the way you take the trade, such as standing up.
- Say one positive word while you click your mouse, such as, "Yes!"

## CONCLUSION

Even the best and brightest traders can face the deep freeze when conditions suddenly change, when roadblocks appear out of nowhere, or when they are unexpectedly off their game. The experience of uncertainty can trigger a chain of events by suddenly releasing negative feelings and thoughts from a past loss or negative experience long forgotten. Overcome by limiting self-talk and feelings, the trader fails to act. When he freezes, he loses confidence. Thus, the cycle of loss begins. Below the surface is a root cause that needs to be uncovered, addressed, and transformed before it triggers more chains of emotional conflict and inaction. Whether this process is accomplished with or without outside professional help, a trader must take steps to address it if he is to avoid or get out of the deep freeze. He needs to prepare—through mental rehearsal—to respond to each trade, regardless of the conditions around him, and follow his rules with confidence and discipline.

---

*Make sure the stories you tell yourself and others support the life you want to have.*

---

CHAPTER 4

# The Price of Holding on to Your Stories

We all have stories that chronicle our lives and why things have turned out the way they have. At first glance, these stories seem harmless enough but the cost of holding on to them can be very high. Instead of explaining why things have turned out the way they are, these harmless stories have the potential to determine how things will be—and how successful we will become in the future.

Some stories are more influential than others. The more we reflect on a particular story, the more powerful that story and its message becomes. The level of detail given to our thoughts determines the depth of the associated feelings. When our feelings have more depth, they have more power to influence our behavior.

If our thoughts about our trading are pleasing, our neurology will support us in following the rules of our trading methodology. However, if the thoughts are disturbing and are attached to actions that go against our rules, a negative pattern of behavior is anchored. When these negative thoughts are repeated, breaking the patterns of behavior that are created becomes more difficult because they are anchored to automatic behavior.

## THE BIG FISH THAT GOT AWAY

Recently, I worked with a trader named Jack, who loved to relate stories in great detail about his ability to precisely forecast market tops and bottoms. Of course, his forecasts made money for everyone but him or so he claimed. "If I could only act on my own advice, I would be a multi-millionaire!" Jack clearly felt that it was important for me to be aware of this detail because he repeated it many times between his stories.

As a trader's coach, I have heard stories like this many times over the years. They are a common theme of people stuck in the loop of over-studying and over-analyzing. These risk-averse analysts would rather have others act on their predictions and bear the risk than take action and responsibility themselves. After the fact, they can cherry pick the stories about being right on forecasts of big trades without assuming the risk themselves. Conveniently, they neglect to include stories about when their predictions were wrong and would have lost money.

Jack desperately needed to encourage himself plus win adulation and applause from others with his stories. Unfortunately, the stories were all that he had to show for his hard work. Jack did work hard—the problem was that he did not work smart. Jack wanted to find a new and innovative shortcut to trading success without having to do what top traders do to become successful.

Sandwiched between his self-promoting trading stories were stories that revealed Jack's other side. These stories revealed the Jack who was anchored in negative behaviors from a self-inflicted, difficult life. These stories told of drug and alcohol abuse, high adventure, macho choices, motorcycle crashes, sleepless nights, poor nutrition, broken relationships, and broken hearts. For Jack, these stories represented conclusive evidence of his unique ability to take risks in other areas of his life. Naturally, he failed to relate this self-sabotaging behavior to his inability to follow his trading rules.

How could a man give up his stories when his self-preservation and identity was so dependent upon them? Jack's stories were extremely interesting initially. Their drama and intensity made his life a high adventure. But when you live in your imagination with such an intense state of emotion, the ordinary becomes boring. Would new stories about a trader following his rules and making money from those rules be enough to sustain his ego?

## MORE FISHY STORIES

Jack's life is not unique. Many traders have stories that explain their failures and their successes. The stories that explain successes are generally positive anchors, even if they result from adversity and loss. Traders who have transformed adversity and loss into success have created their own holy grail or secret formula for success. The traders who have a story justifying their failure to succeed have their own magic formula for continued failure. Let's take a look at six of the generic failure stories:

1. I am the victim of (an unscrupulous, a dishonest, an incompetent, an overpriced, a poorly tested, an under-researched) advisor, newsletter, system, system designer, trading execution service, broker, testing service.
2. I would have been a brilliant success had I not missed that single big trade, which started the whole decline in my trading. It would not have happened (except for the bad day I had, the divorce, the flaw in my system, the sudden and unexpected turn in the market, or any of the victimizing factors in the previous story).
3. My wife/husband/mother/father/significant other has been sabotaging my trading and I have no control over them.
4. I have been permanently traumatized by something that happened in my past (a loss, an act of violence or betrayal, an abandonment).
5. I was trained to deal with a (bull market, bear market, volatile market, static market, floor trading room, institutional trading room, home office, or shared electronic off-the-floor office) and once things changed, I have never been able to find my rhythm again.
6. I was making money hand over fist when I first started trading and something happened (a loss, a change, a mistake, a failure to follow my trading rules) and everything has been downhill since then.

This is a sampling of the generic failure stories that are capable of deeply setting a negative anchor when they are told over and over again. These are not just fish stories; they are fishy stories. They stop ringing true after the second retelling. Professional traders expect to deal with losses and reversals, changes in the markets or trading structure, interruptions, and other negative events that appear on the screen. Instead of using these events or influences as excuses for failure, professional traders look for solutions.

## LETTING GO VERSUS REALLY LETTING GO

Washington Irving, the father of the American short story, was engaged to marry a beautiful young woman who was the love of his life. She died suddenly in the days before their wedding. This tragedy affected him so profoundly that he never married. Later, he confessed to a friend that he was unable to think or talk about it for many years. At the end of his life, he wrote: "Little minds are subdued by misfortune, but great minds rise above it." It is difficult to know whether he was describing himself as the former or the latter. However, the answer may be deduced from the fact that he went on to lead a life that was professionally successful, but personally lonely and unfulfilled. Although Irving appeared to release his tragic story, he never let go of it on the level that really counts: the unconscious level.

A profound tragedy, a painful loss, or a terrifying experience always produces a story. It is a natural human response to an emotionally charged experience to replay the story in our minds giving it a narrative shape and meaning. Like Irving, traders can hold on to their stories even when they give the impression of letting go. Their attachment to their stories can be concealed with smokescreen statements such as:

- You win some; you lose some.
- I don't let anything bother me.
- That stuff happened a long time ago and I don't think about it anymore.
- I can't even remember what happened.
- I'm not the emotional type.
- I just let it roll off me and get on with my trading.

Sometimes, stories run rampant through a trader's mind but he simply does not share them with anyone. He may fear being ridiculed, being vulnerable, or giving his stories more power over him. When he finally releases them into the light of day, they are like dogs barking in the basement. The noise they generate reverberates so loudly that it possesses enormous power while its source is concealed. But the moment the dogs are released from the basement, they show themselves to be relatively harmless creatures that do not bite.

## THE COST OF TURNING NEGATIVE STORIES INTO POSITIVE ONES

Negative stories all share the same power to influence a trader's performance whether they are old stories told *ad nauseam*, hidden stories, or suppressed stories. They all possess the power to excuse a trader from following his rules.

A trader can use the negative narratives to prove that he is a victim and is not responsible for his failures. Armed with his stories, he can prove that it is hopeless to try and that failure is inevitable regardless of your efforts and that life is unpredictable, cruel, and arbitrary. The narratives can be used to prove that people, including himself, cannot be trusted to do the right thing or to fulfill a promise. In short, it is difficult, even next to impossible, to maintain the hard disciplines of a trading master in the face of stories that prove that success is beyond reach. So, if the price of holding on to your stories is this version of 'success,' what is the price of letting go?

- **Fear of being wrong.** Intelligent people like to be right. In fact, our egos are so attached to being right that they would rather be right than successful, healthy, happy, and famous. The highest cost of letting go of your stories is being wrong and, unfortunately, for some traders, the cost is too high.
- **Fear of being vulnerable.** For traders who have been holding on to secret or suppressed stories, letting go of their stories involves the potential for being vulnerable. After all, fear is what prevented them from being revealed in the first place.
- **Fear of the unknown.** If you take a trader's stories away, what will replace them? How will he or she explain the past and present, much less the future? If the stories were negative templates for reality, at least they were predictable. The loss of this security is a high price for many.

The cost of releasing your stories is high indeed, but not as high as the cost of holding on to them. Here are three steps that can be taken to make the letting go much easier to accomplish.

**Step 1.** When the level of pain that results from being right is high enough, letting go of the negative stories supporting your position becomes easier. One way to use this fact is to list the problems that have resulted from the negative story. The first step in letting go of your stories is to identify and focus on the pain that these stories create in your life. In other words, identify the failures, the losses, the anticipation of loss, and holding back from success that these stories have created in your life. Then, really allow yourself to feel the pain caused by being right. Once you have experienced the true cost, it will suddenly become easier to let your stories go.

**Step 2**. When your goal of being successful is powerful enough, letting go can happen quickly. The second step is to replace the goal of being 'right' with the goal of achieving success or happiness, and so on. The important thing is to make this goal a powerful one. It must have detail so you can really see it, feel it, hear it, smell it, and describe it verbally. You must have passion for your new goal(s) and must attach it to a powerful emotion. Without an intense new level of positive feeling and detail, your old stories will still hold their power over you.

**Step 3**. Practice your new positive stories by repeating them to yourself each day. Each time you tell yourself the story it becomes more of a reality. In fact, it takes approximately one month of daily repetition for your neurology to accept a new story and replace the old one. Just remember to tell yourself the story with an intense level of feeling and detail in order to make it real.

## STAYING OUT OF THE STORY

On October 31, 2003, Bethany Hamilton, a 13-year old world-class surfer from Hawaii was attacked by a 14-foot tiger shark. Her left arm was severed just below the shoulder. Miraculously, she survived the attack. Months later, Bethany shocked the world when she was back on her surfboard. The following summer, she placed fifth in the National Surfing Championships and has won a fair number of events since.

To help others overcome their stories, Bethany has written an inspirational book, *Soul Surfer*, about her experience. What put her back on her surfboard after such a terrible attack? Her passion for surfing was stronger than the story. In fact, she is quoted as saying: "I know I have something important to say. Something that people need to hear—but sometimes they get so caught up in the story part that they miss the meaning." Bethany never got caught up in her tragic story.

## RETELLING THE STORY

How can you stop yourself from getting caught up in the stories of your painful, frightening losses? Once you have told yourself the story, listen to what you are actually saying. Really listen. Then ask yourself this question: "Will this story empower me?" If the answer is "Yes" and you feel energized and motivated to succeed and be fulfilled by the story, then go for it. But if you can honestly say that the story will deprive you of energy and the will to move forward, then you need to reframe your story. Like Bethany, you can simply reframe it as an aberration on the way to your passion or you can reframe it as a learning experience.

Recently, many highly successful political and public figures have developed a non-stick surface when caught in messy, compromising situations. What they have learned to do is reframe the story so they become empowered or at the very least absolved from blame. Most of us would be embarrassed to the point of paralysis by the public exposure of these peccadilloes; yet, these public figures move forward with their careers intact because they are not attached to their stories. This talent for reframing should not absolve you from leading a responsible life, but it will protect you from being destroyed by the emotional blows that can cripple your performance.

## CONCLUSION

Every trader's life comes with its fair share of pain that comes from unforeseen, unavoidable, and inevitable losses and failures. The stories that a trader creates from these negative experiences determine his ability to perform and to follow trading rules. If a trader wants to break through the self-imposed barriers to success, he must learn the skill of letting go of these stories. Listening to negative stories, even the ones that have been buried or hidden from others, and reframing them into positive stories or replacing them with empowering goals are the keys to letting go.

But, the best way to release disempowering stories is to learn to keep them from forming in the first place. Become the non-stick trader who reframes each loss as a learning experience and continue moving forward toward your goals.

---

*The choices you make in your trading and in your life will have an impact on whether you are on the right track toward your goals.*

---

CHAPTER 5

# On the Right Track

Why do so many of the people who want to become professional traders find themselves on the wrong track to their destinations? Instead of reaching trading success, they waste their precious time, energy, and money in a long, futile, and tedious journey that leads to a dead end. Here are five major reasons why Trading Hopefuls take the wrong track:

1. They are trying to save time and money by taking shortcuts to success.
2. They want to copy or borrow what they think is the holy grail by using or purchasing someone else's system or method without making it their own.
3. They adopt a trading style that makes money for someone else, but not them because they do not have the same resources.
4. They are "into-wishing" and hoping that they are the exception to the rules of trading and want to change the rules as they are trading.
5. They put their faith in a "trading guru" who promises to turn them into a trader when this trading guru cannot make a living from trading for himself and that is why he is teaching.

As we take a closer look at these wrong tracks to success, ask yourself if you have taken the wrong direction at some point in your trading.

## TRYING TO SAVE MONEY AND TIME

When I ask traders how long it took them to become profitable, they frequently say, "Seven years. But, I'd only count the last two as productive." In other words, they wasted five years taking a short cut. Rather than spending the time and money that was required to become a professional, they looked for the quick and easy solutions. I liken this process of skipping the required education and training to becoming a brain surgeon by reading a book on the subject and buying a steak carving set.

In the five years, not only did these impatient traders lose time and money, they often developed self-sabotage issues that created inconsistencies, irregularities, and unpredictabilities when they finally did become profitable. These self-sabotaging issues will continue to live on in their trading careers until they handle them through coaching or counseling. Three examples of these issues are:

1. **Going into trading without proper preparation**. The short-term result: Experiencing a serious loss and/or a series of losses without adequate preparation. The long-term problems: Fear of loss that prevents a trader from consistently entering or exiting a trade when his system gives him the signals.
2. **Failing to take the time to develop a tested trading system**. The short-term result: An untested system that you do not fully understand and cannot properly use. The long-term problems: Lack of confidence in your system, which leads to inconsistent trading.
3. **Trading before you learn everything you need to learn about the markets**. The short-term result: Getting whip-sawed in the markets because of inadequate education. The long-term problems: Holes in your education make you loss-vulnerable to market variations and more savvy traders.

There are many books on trading and CDs for home studies that will put you on the right track. The problem is: How do you know which ones to pick? It certainly helps to ask those who have been through the struggles and are now successful.

## FOLLOWING SOMEONE ELSE IN HOPES OF TRADING FOR YOURSELF

Some new traders opt to adhere to a mentor-trader in the belief that it will put them on the fast track to trading for themselves.

In this mentoring relationship, the trainee becomes an apprentice to the master, following his system. There are three problems with taking this apprenticeship track without adequate preparation by educating yourself about trading and your own resources:

1. The first problem with this relationship is that the mentor has developed a trading style that works for him, but not necessarily for the apprentice trader. Trading styles are like hairstyles: They are personal. What looks/works for one type of face and one type of hair does not work for another type.
2. Second, you must take into consideration the resources of the individual who you want as a mentor. His education, trading capital, and experience allow him to do what he does. Make sure you know what resources he has, his environment, his background, and his beliefs before you start trying to trade someone else's style. If they do not match your own, you can find yourself moving at light speed from your goals.
3. Finally, in this category, you will find mentors who know a great deal about the markets and do not always remember to fill in the detail of the education you need to follow what they are doing. If you do not have a good base of education about the markets, you might not know the right questions to ask that will make all the difference in your trading results.

Generally speaking, for many people mentorship is a good idea, if you have as a base a good understanding of how the markets work and a traders' business plan. However, you will want to wean yourself off your mentor as soon as you are consistently profitable for at least four months.

## "INTO-WISHING" AND HOPING THAT YOU WILL BE THE EXCEPTION TO THE RULE

The people who become traders in the belief that they can be the exceptions to the rules of successful trading are off on the wrong track from the start. These wishful thinkers believe that they will be successful without getting an education in the technical aspects of trading and without putting together a business plan. Instead, they rely on what they read in the news or what they observe about a particular stock or commodity. If the fundamentals fail them, they might fall back on a ritual, such as holding onto a rabbit's foot and turning three times to the right. "Why not? It worked the last time."

Ultimately, these are the same people who support those who make money in the markets. They have no plan, no training, and no carefully developed, tested system. They become the fodder for the markets, the income-producing prey for the professional traders.

What causes new traders to enter the profession with such a naive, over-inflated view of their invulnerability? To name a few:

- Greed
- Laziness
- Egotism
- Lack of experience

The problem with the "into-wishing" approach to trading is that it guarantees failure in the form of losses. There are no good trading lessons to be derived from it except that it does not work.

## ACQUIRING THE HOLY GRAIL BY USING SOMEONE ELSE'S WORK

Very often a novice will follow a style that is not suited to him because it makes someone else money. As we discussed previously, trading is a very personal and individualized effort. What works brilliantly for one trader may work moderately for another and poorly for a third. Not only will the resources, training, and background of this individual be different from another trader's, his ability to deal with specific time frames, risk, uncertainty, mathematical constructs, boredom, and a host of other personality variables will be different.

If you still believe in Santa, then the search for a holy grail will make sense. Otherwise, the answer to success still resides in the formula:

hard work + intense preparation + adequate capital + psychological preparedness (building discipline and dealing with your sabotage issues in advance of your trading) = trading success.

## HOW DO YOU KNOW WHEN YOU ARE ON THE WRONG TRACK?

Your trading has an automatic feedback system to tell you when you are on the wrong track. It is called inconsistent results. When you are losing more money than you are making from your trading, something is not right with your trading and you are going in the wrong direction. There are only four reasons for your inconsistency. You do not have:

- Enough education
- Time and or money for being a professional trader
- A system which makes money under current market conditions
- The ability to follow the rules of your system

There is another signal that you are on the wrong track that is not as definitive as poor performance. When you are experiencing emotional discomfort in your trading, you are on the wrong track. If you are plagued with fear, boredom, or the feeling that you need to get more excitement into your trading, you are also on the wrong track. Adequate physical, emotional, and educational preparation will allow you to trade with confidence and a sense that things are going along in the right direction.

## CONCLUSION

There is no express train to success in trading that bypasses the stops of preparation, hard work, and commitment. It is true that there are some excellent strategies that can cut the time and the amount of loss you will experience as you travel toward trading success, but they, too, require planning, preparation, and the commitment of resources. Fortunately, once you understand the requirements for becoming a professional trader, you will be able to read the roadmap to success and avoid all the dead ends and detours along the way.

---

*What happy thoughts will you focus on today?*

---

CHAPTER 6

# Motivators for a Down Day

Even highly successful traders have down days when their physical and emotional energy level is so low that they would rather just stay in bed. As difficult as these down days are to deal with, they are an ever-present part of the human experience. Each trader has a finite number of trading days in his career, and therefore the issue of down days is relevant as each trading day counts regardless of whether you make the most of it.

Because they are common, down days can make the difference between being profitable and losing money in the markets. It is important to learn how to limit their number and how to handle them when they do occur. To accomplish this, it is important to develop an understanding of what causes down days and find possible solutions.

## THE LOW ENERGY TRADER

Richard has a lot of down days. Lately, half of this 35-year-old trader's week could be described as a down day. On low-energy days, his work is performed at half speed. He thinks slowly and avoids doing anything challenging. He coasts through the day until dinnertime, hoping that he does not make a major mistake or miss a great opportunity. Recently, his wife became so concerned about his energy level that she forced him to get a major physical checkup. His doctor could find nothing physically wrong but could not provide any changes to stop the down days. This was his situation when he called me for help. The first thing was to isolate the cause.

## Energy-Sappers

Most of our down days result from low physical or emotional energy. Since our minds and bodies are interdependent, when one system is down, the other system seems to go down as well. If we are depressed emotionally, we often find that our bodies will also seem to lose energy. Many people who are physically sick often become depressed or feel emotionally fragile. The good news is that lifting one system often provides improvement to the other system.

**The Physical Causes** Before you look for emotional energy sappers, eliminate the possible physical causes. And, always check with your doctor before implementing a new program. Major illnesses such as cancer, kidney and heart disease, diabetes, myasthenia gravis, or multiple sclerosis have symptoms where down days become progressively worse as the body's level of energy drops. Physical examinations are designed to detect these major systemic or organic problems. Unfortunately, physical examinations rarely catch the more subtle problems that result in lost vitality. Physical Energy Sappers include:

- **Poor nutrition**—A bad diet is one of the greatest energy robbers for traders. Low protein consumption, combined with a lack of B vitamins from whole grains, vegetables, meats, and nuts and certain minerals such as potassium can cause a serious shortage of energy. Refined foods and alcohol can destroy and displace these essential elements.
- **Low blood sugar**—Blood sugar levels have a profound effect on your daily energy level. Blah days can permanently disappear for some traders once their blood sugar is stabilized. Traders who rely on sugar and caffeine for a quick fix during the day actually make their energy problem worse as sugar and caffeine destroy the B vitamins that are so vital to making energy.
- **Stress and low adrenal function**—Under prolonged stress, your adrenal glands can become exhausted. When that happens, you will feel down and have little energy. You may wake up four hours into the night's rest and be unable to get back to sleep. In the morning, you feel even more exhausted. To get your adrenal glands functioning, eliminate the processed foods and alcohol, take vitamin B5 (Pantothenic Acid), get uninterrupted sleep, and reduce your stress.
- **Poor sleep**—A good night's rest is essential for continuous energy and vitality. If you get to bed at different times each night and fail to get adequate calcium/magnesium in your diet, the sleep pattern that you

are establishing is not healthy and predictable. The result will be a lot of down days.

- **Excessive drinking and drug use**—Useless, blah mornings typically follow nights when drugs and alcohol are overdone.
- **Allergies**—Allergies change the production and function of the brain's neurotransmitters. Sudden increases in pollen or mold levels can make a trader feel like he is fighting his way through a haze all day.
- **Lack of exercise**—If you do not get adequate exercise, you will begin to feel sluggish and find it difficult to concentrate.

**Strategies for Pulling Out of a Down Day Due to Physical Causes** Physical causes are the easiest to address and their strategies are usually simple although they may not be what you want to hear. You may simply have to forget about trading on a particular down day and take care of your body. Only you know whether you are down because of something you ate, drank, or took into your body.

**If the problem is exhaustion from a lack of sleep**, forget about trading. Take the day off and get to bed. If it is not possible to take the day off, work but do not trade. Keep your stress levels low and take good care of yourself. There is no cure for this day but rest.

**If you are merely tired, but not to the point of exhaustion**, take a 10- to 15-minute catnap. This will revive you for several hours. Stay away from carbohydrates at lunch or you will not be able to stay awake in the afternoon. If your energy is marginal, stick to doing things you can do automatically. Sometimes, just keeping going will actually begin to rev up the old engines. However, a good night's sleep is required tonight.

**If you had too much to drink** and feel severely depleted, replace nutrients and hydrate. Metabolism of alcohol requires the body to use its store of salt, water, and various B vitamins. You will feel better when these nutrients are replaced. A teaspoon of salt in a tall glass of water with a good multi-vitamin and a small meal can work wonders for your energy.

**A lack of activity** can create down days. Get up from your desk and find a way to take a brisk walk or get to the gym for a quick workout. You will feel recharged as a result. A word of caution: Do not overdo it!

**Adrenal Exhaustion** is the cause of a high percentage of down days. Stress, emotional scenes, lack of sleep, a bad diet, and worry can exhaust your adrenals and leave you feeling down. Severe muscle pain in the neck and shoulders may also develop. This one-day emergency regimen may be helpful: Pantothenic Acid (vitamin B5), electrolyte builders, no caffeine or sugar, and no stress for the first half of the day.

**The Emotional Causes** If you recognize the source of your down days from the list of physical causes, you may realize that correcting negative physical patterns can dramatically improve the quality of your trading days. However, this strategy may not eliminate your down days. In fact, determining the physical causes of your lost energy may merely clear the deck for you to handle the underlying emotional causes of your down days. Emotional energy sappers include:

- **Pessimism and Depression.** Depression is probably the number one emotional cause of down days. In order to understand depression, pessimism needs to be understood first. Pessimism is the pervasive belief in the power of the negative to control your life. The pessimist universalizes all negative experiences but deems all positive outcomes as temporary up-ticks in a down-tick world.
- **Negative Emotional States.** No matter what emotional label you give it—such as fear, anger, or sadness—whenever you feel emotionally down you deplete your body's energy. The same process you used to create these downward spiraling emotional states is what you can use to get yourself into a positive mode. Before an emotion, there is self-talk and before self-talk there are pictures. Change the pictures, change the self-talk, and you will change the emotional state. So instead of creating a negative picture of some bad thing happening to you, create a picture of something good that can happen. Instead of saying negative words to yourself, translate those words to a positive statement.
- **Broken promises.** When we fail to live up to our commitments and promises to others, we end up feeling badly about ourselves. We can also lose trust in ourselves when we fail to fulfill our promises. This effect is especially powerful when failure to follow trading rules or strategy rules results in a significant loss. The result can lead to feelings of hopelessness and being out of control.

***Outside Influences*** If a trader takes better care of his physical and emotional health, the number of down days in his life can be limited. However, other causes for down days are completely outside of a trader's control. For example:

- **The weather**—Changes in the weather can create down days. Geographic regions that experience long spells of gloomy weather also experience the highest rates of depression and suicide. Sunlight appears to influence mood and a sense of wellbeing.

- **Bad news**—No one is immune to bad news. It could be almost anything: a friend dies, a spouse loses a job, a bad result from a medical test, or a catastrophe that affects others and us. Down days may follow as a result.
- **Isolation**—Traders who work from home without much human contact can have down days simply from a lack of social interaction.
- **Unpleasant Social Exchanges**—When someone decides to unload his misery on you, it can leave you feeling down. Unpleasant exchanges can come without warning. Nevertheless, the rest of your day can spiral downward because of it.

**Strategies for Pulling Out of a Down Day Due to Emotional Causes** Knowing some key information is vital to pulling yourself out of a downward tailspin.

***Are you an introvert or an extrovert?*** An extrovert gains energy by being around other people. An introvert builds energy by being alone and away from others. How do you fill up your emotional engines?

**Strategy One:** If you are an extrovert, get on the phone and talk with someone who likes to hear from you or find a place where people congregate and join in the conversation.

**Strategy Two:** If you are an introvert, find your own cave and shut the door so that you can rebuild your emotional energy. Fifteen minutes of peace and quiet is often enough to bring you back to a state of *emotional equilibrium*.

***Are you a pessimist or optimist?***

**Strategy Three:** If you are an optimist, analyze what pulled you into a down day. Mentally list the positive things that have happened and all of your proudest achievements. Picture the last time you pulled yourself out of a bad situation. Congratulate yourself for your creativity and courage and imagine how you can use this to reverse the situation! Fill up with a sense of power and take action. Reward yourself afterward.

**Strategy Four:** If you are a pessimist, you may need a friend to help you. This should be someone who believes in you and has known you long enough to remind you of all that you have achieved in your life. As a pessimist, you may find yourself piling bad news on top of bad news, making life seem hopeless.

An effective way out of this trap is to use a reality check to balance the scales. Look realistically at what has happened and ask yourself if this experience marks the end of the world. Has this problem ever been solved by others? Have you been able to resolve experiences of this kind in the past? Are you the only person who has ever experienced this situation? Once you have acknowledged that this one negative experience is just a blip on the radar screen of life, you are ready to pile on the positive.

List all of the positives in your life. This exercise may seem unpleasant and you may feel resistance. As the list grows, the scales in your unconscious will begin to tip in favor of the positive. If you find this difficult, call a friend and ask him or her to list positive things in your life. A true pessimist often needs help in tipping the scales.

***What has pulled you out of a down day in the past?***

**Strategy five:** Here are four strategies that have helped others. Any one of them could work for you.

1. **Rewards as Treats.** Some traders begin to pull out of a down day when they reward themselves. A reward unconsciously reminds us of a time when we were happy or when we felt good about ourselves. Sometimes, a reward simply provides enough pleasure that our brains increase the level of neurotransmitters. These rewards are not for anything well done, but for just being alive and on the planet.
    - Enjoy chocolate or a dessert that is rich and decadent. However, if food is an addiction for you, this reward could make things worse in your life.
    - Watch a movie (with popcorn) that makes you laugh, cry, or feel intensely alive.
    - Stay away from needlessly violent, sad, and depressing films.
    - Read a good book with a cup of tea or coffee. Put your feet up and turn the telephone off. Make it a great read that pulls you into a different world.
    - Watch your favorite team or hit some balls at a golf range.
    - Visit or call someone you have not talked to and really miss. Make certain this individual will be so pleased and surprised to hear from you that you will feel great about the call.
2. **Rewards as Incentives.** Some traders need incentives to pull themselves out of a slump. If this strategy has worked for you in the past, find a reward that adds energy, motivation, or excitement to your day. If you suddenly become energized by the

thought that you are going to reward yourself with a special gift, set a goal or limit and follow through!

3. **Laughter as Medicine.** For some of us, being able to laugh is all that is needed to recharge our batteries. Laughter can be a great and inexpensive cure for a down day.
4. **Motivational CDs, books, spiritual resources, and so on.** In the past, have you responded to the motivational messages from others? If so, tape messages on your computer and read them when you start to feel yourself slipping into a hole. Read passages from spiritual books, listen to motivational CDs, or read the biography of any person whose life has inspired you.

**Strategy Six:** Call a person who will listen and pull you back up. Just talking with this individual is often enough to get you back on track. If a bad encounter with someone has destroyed your self-confidence, this person is the one who will understand and pump you back up with evidence of your worthiness.

**Strategy Seven.** Do one thing that always pulls you out of a spiral. Each of us has a favorite activity that always pulls us back. You simply have to remember what it is. Since trading when you are down is a waste of time, you may as well take an hour or two to do the one thing that will salvage the rest of the day.

## TWO FINAL CAVEATS

Regardless of what has caused you to fall into a down day, the return trip will be faster, easier, and more painless if you have done the preventive work outlined in this article. If you are physically and mentally healthy, the down day will have a softer landing and there will be less to overcome in getting you back aloft. The strategies for getting out of a down day are much more difficult to implement if you wait to think of them when you are in the middle of a bad day. Do not wait until you are in dire straits to remember who to call or what to do.

Now, review this chapter and highlight any of the ideas that ring true for you and/or have worked in the past. Then make a list to follow next time you are having a down day. Changing even one thing can make a difference.

## CONCLUSION

Pulling out of a down day requires that you act swiftly while you still have some semblance of control. You need to be able to draw from your experience and body of information that consists of what you know about yourself and how you got into this downward spiral to begin with. Like all great questions, the answers are inside you already—you just need to know where to look.

---

*Detailing your senses toward the outcome you want is the passion that will run your engine.*

---

CHAPTER 7

# The Internally Motivated Trader Part 1

Do you know what needs to be done to be successful, but cannot seem to force yourself to do it? Instead, do you find reasons and excuses to shift responsibility and blame? Do you feel worried, angry, and frustrated? Why do you feel badly about yourself? What is happening here?

If you are having trouble maintaining your trading success, you may not be trading from the right set of motivations. Like most traders, you may not even be aware of the forces that propel you each day to succeed or fail.

Are you sitting at your computer from 6:30 a.m. until 11:30 p.m. motivated by:

- Fear that you will not be able to make your next mortgage payment?
- A burning desire to buy a new house or new expensive toy?
- The need to show your in-laws that you are able to make it as a trader?
- The need to move into your own office downtown?

If one of these sounds like your motivation, you are not motivating yourself for long-term success. When your motivation comes from forces outside of yourself, your life will be spent solving short-term problems or needs. It could be satisfying the desire to own or possess a particular thing, meeting the expectations of others, or responding to external conditions. But, once the external and/or short-term goals are met, your level of motivation will evaporate like fog in a hot sun leaving you motivationally adrift until another emergency occurs or you find another problem to solve or yearning to satisfy.

## THE EXTERNALLY MOTIVATED TRADER

I have seen a number of traders who have been working from the wrong kind of motivation. Several years back, Tom reached his trading peak when he earned enough money in a few highly successful trades to move his family into their dream home. He was also able to put money in the bank and pay off the loans needed to set up his trading business. Since then, he has struggled to maintain his momentum while responding to one crises or financial demand after another.

"I want to do better," he told me. "Why?" I asked. Tom did not have a good answer to that question and that is where the problem is. I am not saying that he did not have reasons to want to succeed. He explained that his wife was not well enough to hold down a full-time job after a bout with cancer and that their medical bills were a constant problem to resolve. He was also eager to prove to his family that they were wrong in not supporting him in his trading. He wanted to show them that he was not only financially secure, but that he was wealthy by their standards.

In his mid-thirties, Tom is an intelligent, educated, and attractive man. However, when he was growing up, he was not a socially successful teenager. In school, his penchant for mathematics and science made him the butt of ridicule and bullying. Now, standing over six feet tall and having worked out with weights for years, Tom no longer has the look of someone who would attract a bully. However, he still bears the scars of feeling powerless and unappreciated. Twenty years later, Tom is still responding to the demands and expectations of others and is out of touch with the things that are meaningful to him.

## THE LOW-DOWN ON MOTIVATION

What is so important about a trader's motivation? Traders who have had long, successful careers are nearly always internally motivated. They are successful because they are inspired to act by their own hidden agenda, which may even be unknown to them. Traders who are internally motivated may not necessarily win more fights than they lose, but when they hit those inevitable bumps in the road, they have the involuntary internal muscle that propels them back up onto their feet and into the fray.

Traders who are externally motivated are moved forward by circumstances and/or by the demands and expectations of others. They want to be successful because of the response that others will have to their success. They measure their own worth through the eyes of others. If they see success as the source of money, security, independence, and prestige, they are motivated to create these conditions because they want others to feel good about them.

If they want to be successful to avoid the pain of failure, loss, powerlessness, or embarrassment, they are still being motivated by their need to gain recognition from the outside world. If they are motivated to succeed in order to solve a problem or to even a score, once the problem is solved and the score is settled, the motivation disappears.

## THE SOURCE OF THE PROBLEM

Where does internal motivation come from? It would be wonderful to say that internally motivated people always come from strong, supportive, and stable families and that externally motivated people always develop from dysfunctional homes and/or instability. However, this is not necessarily the case.

After many years of working with traders, most of the externally motivated people that I have worked with have come from homes that were within the range of normal. In fact, some of the most internally motivated traders emerged from the most challenging personal circumstances—from situations that would make you wonder how anyone could achieve or succeed after experiencing their early lives!

Even the most well-meaning (if misguided) parents can turn out externally motivated children if they overprotect them, criticize them, or demean them. They can also fail to give their children responsibilities or choices and allow them the freedom to accomplish and/or fail. What children take from their early experiences and from their own unique genetic makeup can become a toxic combination of three dominant and motivation-robbing attitudes:

- **Powerlessness**— "I don't have the power or influence over the important things in my life. I am a victim."
- **Pessimism**— "It's hopeless anyhow. I'll never have what I want. I am a victim."
- **Passivity**— "I don't know what I want or need. I don't deserve it. I can't get it for myself. I have to depend upon others and the outside world to provide what I want and need. I am a victim."

These attitudes are often so deep-seated that the externally motivated trader may not be consciously aware of them. Regardless of their successes later on in life, these traders are never in touch with the things that have brought them the most satisfaction, pleasure, or joy. They fail to enjoy the process of what they do. Instead, they solve short-term problems and seek to gain the regard of others since their own self-regard is low.

## Low Self-Esteem

Low self-esteem is the single most significant piece of the puzzle. Without a sense of worthiness, the externally motivated trader does:

- what he does for others or to satisfy external demands
- not do the things for himself that he should do
- not know what he really wants or needs or feels

Unfortunately, satisfying the expectations of others or meeting short-term needs is not a powerful enough purpose to motivate a trader to do all of the things that he needs to do to be successful.

## Failing to Follow Through

When Don left our weekend coaching session, he was psychologically pumped and full of enthusiasm. "I can't tell you how much this has meant to me," he said as he left. "I can't wait to get started." He was referring to the processes and assignments that we had developed to bring him to the next level of success in his trading.

Generally, after a coaching session, a client will take off like a rocket. In the past, I have seen traders double and triple their profits within weeks. Many of them have exceeded the million-dollar mark many times over. But, occasionally, a client will fail to follow through. This result is quite unusual because I screen clients for their level of motivation. It is not worth my time or their money to go through this process if they are not going to do the work. So, it was a great surprise to me when Don failed to follow through.

What would cause a trader to spend a considerable amount of money and time to bring about a new level of success and then drop the ball? Why would he be unwilling to do the things that are necessary to reach his goals? There are some very good answers:

- They really are not his goals, regardless of what he may say.
- He does not know what he really wants.
- He is trying to please someone else and not himself.
- He has failed to take responsibility for his own wellbeing.
- Money and a high level of success are not important.

### Taking Responsibility

Failing to take responsibility is directly related to the three motivation-sapping attitudes: powerlessness, pessimism, and passivity. All three of these forces are predicated on the assumption that the individual is ultimately not responsible for his own wellbeing. He is at the mercy of life's forces and is not the shaper of his own fate. This position offers a convenient way out for the individual.

The problem with being externally motivated is that you must find someone to blame or shift responsibility onto. When you enter a coaching relationship, the responsibility is ultimately with the one who is being coached. He is the one who must follow through and do the work.

For this reason, great athletes are always internally motivated. No one has to tell them to practice eight hours a day. They blame no one for the pain, for the hard work, for the sacrifices, or for the ultimate results. When they are coached, they take full responsibility for following through on their coach's instructions. They are doing what they love to do, they believe that they are winners, and that they deserve to win. These are the internal motivators that propel them over the finish line to success.

## CONCLUSION

Traders who fail to follow through to do what it takes to be successful are often externally motivated. Rather than being motivated by inner goals and a sense of self-worth, externally motivated traders may be driven to make money in the markets to please others or to solve short-term needs. Unfortunately, when the needs are met or the demands to meet them become too high to justify the cost, the trader will easily lose the wind in his sails.

---

*Once your engine is sparked with passion, it is easier to keep it headed in the right direction.*

---

CHAPTER 8

# The Internally Motivated Trader Part 2

So, you have come to the conclusion that you are an externally motivated trader. Instead of acting from your own needs and desires, you respond to the needs of others and the demands of circumstances. You have also come to the decision that you no longer want to be driven by external motivations. You want to reach the highest level of trading success that you are capable of reaching without being held back by the wrong kind of motivations.

Excellent! But, what can you do to change these deep-seated motivational issues? Time travel is not possible yet. It is impossible to go back in time to reverse the messages that you were given or to erase the experiences that created your sources of motivation, which in turn, affects your sense of self-worth. Or, is it?

## SETTING THE TRAP

In my opinion, one of the greatest advances in the study of the human condition is the development of our understanding of how we form our self-image. Why is our self-image so important? That deep, unconscious, and indelible picture that we have of ourselves is such a powerful force in our lives that it becomes the template for our future attitudes, actions, and outcomes. And, that holds a lot of power over your trading future.

Now, we know that the process of creating that self-image begins with a highly charged experience or verbal exchange. The more negative the experience is the more charge it has, giving it more power to affect us. Also, the younger we are when the experience occurs, the more lasting and powerful the impression will be on our psyche.

Once the emotionally charged or influential experience has occurred, we talk to ourselves about it, applying our own spin to the story of what has just happened. Our interpretation of this experience is critical to what will happen next. For example:

If we tell ourselves that a bad experience was merely a fluke or an accident and nothing to be upset over, we may actually move past it. We may even lay down a picture of ourselves as being lucky to survive with minor damage. Or, we may think that we are pretty strong, brave, and capable for handling such a bad situation so well. But, if we tell ourselves that the same bad experience was embarrassing, shameful, or terrible and that we are unlucky and powerless, we will feel like a victim making us vulnerable to more bad things happening to us. In this case, the picture that we create of ourselves in our minds will be one of powerlessness and vulnerability.

Once the picture is created, we lay down the voiceover, which can sound like this:

- "I am so stupid."
- "I can't talk in public without embarrassing myself."
- "I can never do anything right."
- "I can never succeed for very long. I always fail in the end."
- "The markets hate me. They always take back more than they give."
- "I can never keep up a winning streak."

Notice how absolute these statements are. They are filled with the words "always" and "never". They universalize the experience in the same way that pessimists do. In *Learned Optimism*, Dr. Martin Seligman's landmark book on optimism and pessimism, we learn how pessimists universalize each negative experience to prove that the world is an unhappy and unlucky place for them. These two dynamic processes, the pessimistic worldview and the creation of an unconscious self-image, intersect to create a motivation-sapping self-image. The pessimist has a bad experience that he universalizes and creates an indelible unconscious image that has a pessimistic interpretation for the voice over. Then, this image helps him to interpret all future experiences and shapes his reaction to them.

Each new experience only proves the validity of his picture of himself and his life, reinforcing the pessimistic view and its hold over him. If an experience is in perfect alignment with his image of himself and how life is for him, he gets to say, "See, that's how it is." Should an experience contradict his picture of the way things are, he gets to say, "This is the exception."

You can see how easy it is to become trapped in the prison of a negative self-image. Even if you tell yourself that you want to be successful, you are actually being motivated by unconscious attitudes and feelings. If your self-image portrays you as a victim, you will continually view yourself as not accountable for your happiness and success. Luck and circumstance will always be in the driver's seat and you will unconsciously see yourself as the passenger who is merely along for the ride.

## A TRADER AT EFFECT

A trader named Ben was externally motivated but wanted to change the source of his motivation. Everything was going well for Ben until he turned six and started school. He was raised in a happy and stable family, but soon discovered that his happy and sheltered home life left him vulnerable to attacks and manipulations of a trio of aggressive and unhappy classmates. These three little miscreants took one look at the sweet and innocent kid and instantly identified him as their prey. For the next year, they told him that he was fat, ugly, and stupid. They teased and taunted him, until this once happy and self-confident child could barely stand himself. Of course, the truth was that he was a very intelligent, beautiful, and slender young child. But, he did not know the facts. He knew only what he was told. His parents went to the school and pleaded with the teacher to stop the attacks but they were told that there was nothing that could be done.

If we fast-forward thirty-some years, we find Ben trading at home, fighting to stay ahead of the bank, the tax man, and the bill collector. He is struggling with his trading and unable to understand why he feels so powerless in his efforts to make headway. What Ben does not understand is that his sense of powerlessness, hopelessness, and passivity are a direct result of his self-image. A large part of that image was forged in the first grade classroom and playground.

What Ben tells himself intellectually is that he is working as hard as he can and that he is committed to becoming a truly successful trader. But, Ben's little voice tells him that whenever something negative happens, the real cause of the problem is that he is unworthy and incapable of creating success. As a result, he looks to the outside to find the solution.

Another result of Ben's low self-image is that he is not certain why he is trading. He is certainly not doing it for himself since he does not really enjoy the process and does not believe that he should be successful. Part of him is doing it because he thinks it will please his wife and will give her bragging rights within her social circle.

## WHAT IS DONE MAY ACTUALLY BE UNDONE (SOMETIMES)

Once you understand how the original motivation-sapping image is created, you will understand the process of reversing those steps by replacing the negative image with one that promotes feelings of worthiness, self-assurance, and the resilience needed to handle setbacks.

However, there is one important caveat. This process requires that you be motivated enough to do the work and follow through. Externally motivated people often lack the necessary level of self-regard to put forth the effort, and they often lack the optimism to keep them going when the outcome looks distant and difficult to achieve. For some traders, this Catch-22 is too difficult to overcome by themselves. If you feel that you cannot handle this process by yourself, it is a wise trader who seeks out help and support.

### Stage One—Changing Your Negative Self-Perceptions

Here are the nine major steps that are required to reverse specific negative self-images that create external motivations:

1. **Identify the negative image.** This begins the process and may be the hardest to accomplish on your own. What picture do you carry around of an experience or situation that makes you feel powerless? You may have many of these, but you want to start with the earliest one. Like a tangled net, if you pick out the prime thread and unravel it, the others will soon follow.
2. **Re-experience the experience.** Even if the experience is a really painful one, it is important that you get in touch with what it is that you have created as an indelible memory.
3. **Listen to your self-talk.** Along with the picture of the experience, listen to the words that you use to describe the experience. How did you define your life as a result of this experience? What did you say to yourself?
4. **Identify the emotion.** What is the feeling that you get from this experience? Is it pain, loss, embarrassment, powerlessness, humiliation, anger? Let yourself feel the feeling.
5. **Change the outcome of the experience. Rewrite the action.** Once you have identified the negative image, remind yourself that this experience only exists in your memory. Therefore, you have the ability to

rewrite it as you please. How would you like this experience to work out for you? What outcome would give you a sense of control, of self-esteem, of success?

6. **Rewrite the voiceover.** Along with the new image and outcome, you need to rewrite your self-talk providing your interpretation of the new experience.
7. **Create a new emotion.** To accompany the image and the voiceover, you need to pump up the emotional volume for the experience. It is essential to have a powerfully felt emotion to go with this new image. Emotion is the charge that burns the image into your unconscious mind. Without it, this new image will not have enough energy to replace the old one.
8. **Imagine the new image.** The power that the old image has had over you has been reinforced by the many times it was replayed in your mind. Now, you need to replay this new image over and over in your mind in its place with the voiceover and the powerful emotion. You must repeat this exercise every day for a minimum of 30 days, at least once a day. It is preferable to do it in the morning and in the evening when your mind is cleared of other thoughts.
9. **Get help.** If you're like most people, this process may be beyond your ability. If this is the case, work with someone who has the experience to help you identify and change the problem(s).

When done correctly and with committed follow-through, this process is amazingly effective. It will help recreate the image you have of yourself and, without directly addressing them, will begin to change your attitudes about life. You will begin to feel more energetic, more powerful, and more directed. Soon, you will be ready to take the next step in changing your source of motivation.

Ben decided to work with me. Since his young predatory classmates had largely formed his self-image, the process required him to change the old scripts where his hecklers attempted to convince him that he was fat, ugly, and stupid. In his new script, Ben decided that the most empowering experience for him would be to bring in a team of experts who publicly proclaimed that he was handsome, slim, and brilliant. His classmates were shamed into apologizing to him and admitting that they were wrong. Ben's new voiceover proclaimed him to be handsome, slim, brilliant, and king of the situation. He attached powerful emotion to his new image.

## Stage Two—Redefining your Goals

Once you have purged your mind of its motivation-sapping images and replaced them with positive, empowering ones, it is time to take the next step. Now, you have an engine that can get you where you want to go. The question is: Where do you want to go?

This next step may be very easy. But, if you have been operating on external motivation, you may never have been in touch with the things that are really important to you. When faced with a blank page, you may feel anxious, confused, or just plain blank. Once again, you may need to seek outside help or support. Do not feel that you are off track if you seek help. In my experience, internally motivated traders are the ones most likely to look for outside help in reaching their goals because they are highly motivated and will employ all the available resources to reach them.

## CONCLUSION

The first step for traders who want to replace their career-sabotaging external motivation with internal motivation is to reverse the process that created the negative self-images in the first place. A new empowering self-image will make it possible for a trader to believe in himself enough to feel that he is worthy and able to reach his goals. The next step is to find out what those goals really are.

PART II

# Letting Go of Emotional States

*When you let go of fear, you let go of stress. When you let go of stress you have the fertilizer to grow anything.*

CHAPTER 9

# Letting Go of Fear

Since 9–11, our world has been dominated by a sense of vulnerability. The news media is constantly churning out stories about dangers in our surroundings, in our food, in our schools, and in virtually every arena of our lives. This barrage of fear messages from our environment translates into an increase in fear thoughts that intrude in our day-to-day lives.

How does this pervasive sense of vulnerability affect a trader when fear is one of his greatest enemies? Does this increase in a trader's level of fear begin to affect his bottom line? And if so, how can a trader learn to let go of fear?

## FEAR, DREAD, ANXIETY, NERVOUSNESS

These are really the four horsemen of the apocalypse: fear, dread, anxiety, and nervousness. They ride into our lives together, spreading destruction in their path. Rather than being discrete and separate emotions, they are simply extensions of the state of being afraid. Dread is the feeling that many of us awaken to in the middle of the night or first thing in the morning when we think about the issues and problems we must face that day. Anxiety is that constant and low level of fear that has no specific face. And nervousness is that unsettling feeling that fills us as we approach a situation or a person we fear. Fear has many faces and these are just a few of them.

These feelings are all part of the same thing, and when we learn about one of them, we are simply learning about another facet of fear.

## The Fearful Trader

What is the effect of fear on a trader? A fearful trader sees and hears only a fraction of the information that comes his way. As a result, he makes decisions in the dark. To compound the problem, fear slows down his reaction time, so that he may be reacting too late to incomplete information. To explore the problem, a major corporation studied the effects of fear and intimidation on the transmission of important directives within its organization. They were greatly surprised at the results. From the president to his vice presidents, the message lost some of its impact. From the vice presidents to their general managers, it lost more of its substance. By the time this same directive had reached the workers at their desks, very little of the original message survived. The reason that each successive listener had lost so much of the message was that he felt intimidated by his superior and was thus unable to concentrate on the actual message.

Innumerable studies have confirmed the fact that when people get nervous, they get stupid. Test anxiety renders brilliant students unable to think. Nervousness prevents traders from accessing their creative intelligence and ability to problem solve. It clouds our judgment, rendering us helpless, like a deer immobilized by the oncoming car lights. And fear takes energy away from the very act of solving problems and achieving results.

In an August 2004 interview in the *Atlantic Monthly*, David Allen, the guru of personal organization said that we awaken at 3:00 a.m. in a state of anxiety over all the things that we have not done. He says that the anxiety about these undone tasks creates "an all-pervasive stress factor whose source can't be pinpointed"* and that these things stay on our mind, creating stress, sapping energy, and preventing us from doing the very things we are worrying about and fearing. His solution, which he outlines in his bestselling book, *Getting Things Done, The Art of Stress-Free Productivity*, is to get things off your mind through a series of simple techniques that allow you to get them done rapidly. The more they stay on your mind, the less you are able to concentrate on completing them. Instead of managing stuff, priorities, and thoughts about getting things done, you manage action.

---

*Fallows, James. 2004. "Organize Your Life!" *Atlantic Magazine*. July/August. http://www.theatlantic.com/magazine/archive/2004/07/organize-your-life/3455/.

## The Four Horsemen of Letting Go of Fear

Here are four steps toward letting go of fear.

**1. Taking Action** In his book, David Allen points out one of the first and most important keys to letting go of fear: Taking action. Another giant in the field of human development, Tony Robbins, is also a big proponent of taking action as the antidote to going in circles in your life. Both of these men recommend the same strategy—that you have to decide what is the next step to take, and then commit to it and take it. That step should be small, in fact, very small, and immediately achievable. Examples of taking a small, achievable step are:

- Looking up a phone number
- Making a phone call
- Locating an address or a piece of information
- Sending off a letter or email
- Buying a simple filing system at an office supply house
- Cleaning off one corner of your desk
- Starting a file in your computer

Taking even the smallest action reduces your level of fear regardless of its source, or the level of risk involved, or the level of fear you are experiencing. Fear drops away as you take the smallest action for two reasons:

- Taking action removes or reduces thoughts of the problem
- Taking action immediately starts solving the problem

Stop thinking or limit the amount of thinking you do about a problem by writing down the next action you must take and then taking it. Thinking about a problem uses up energy and sets up roadblocks to solving the problem, thereby increasing your fear.

The problem for a lot of traders is that the dread level is so high that they need help in overcoming that hurdle. That leads me to my second key to letting go of fear.

**2. Building in Rewards** I reward myself all day long for accomplishing things I dread doing. Like everyone else, I have things I would rather avoid but I have trained myself to reward myself for taking action. So, instead of focusing on the thing I dread, I focus on the reward. Thus, I am rewarding myself continually, while reinforcing in my neurology the association between doing things I dread and getting rewards. This powerful conditioning allows me to accomplish things that leave most people paralyzed with apprehension.

Some tips for producing the best results are as follows. The bigger the fear and dread, the more compelling should be the reward. It is a question of energy and momentum. You have to overcome inertia with more energy than it takes to move an already moving object. But, if that object is moving in the opposite direction, it takes even more energy. If you are actively avoiding doing something you dread, then you will need to put more energy into the system to reverse your negative movement. That increased energy comes in the form of a bigger reward, which represents a larger incentive for us to reverse our direction.

Think of the thing you dread the most. For many people, the things they fear the most involve dealing with other people because these exchanges can result in humiliation and/or rejection. Right after these fears come the fear of loss and pain and the unknown. If you are forced to deal with the fear of these potential elements, you will need to build in some powerful incentives to motivate you.

So, start developing a list of rewards and incentives. Begin your list with the smallest rewards and go right up to the most outrageous ones. The promise of a major reward after tackling a major fear has helped countless traders to overcome roadblocks in their lives. Once you have done something you fear once, and you have rewarded yourself, you are less anxious the next time you must face the same fear.

**3. Clearing Your Mind** This step is probably the single most effective step in managing fear. The act of letting go of fear by clearing your mind is not something you can do just by willing it to be so. It is a skill that comes from practice, and develops over time after a serious commitment to the process.

The only effective path I know to letting go is through the mind-clearing practices of meditation and/or prayer. Although prayer may be a useful tool for some, in my experience meditative practices produce the most effective results in letting go. Most meditative practices will allow you to let go of thoughts of fear, anxiety, dread, and nervousness.

Meditation is the art of stilling the mind by focusing on the breath or a single sound like "ah" (this sound is known as a mantra). Once the mind quiets down, fearful thoughts lose their power and they simply float away. The result is that the mind fails to send messages to your adrenals to release cortisol and adrenaline each and every time you have a fleeting fearful thought during the course of the day. Not only do you no longer react in a knee-jerk fashion to the steady stream of fear thoughts, but you soon discover that you have fewer and fewer of these fear thoughts. Instead, your mind stays clear, you can think, and you have total access to your creative intelligence.

**4. Seeking Help** Sometimes, the solution to a problem lies outside of us. When your level of fear rises above the manageable level, one of the fastest and most effective ways to reduce that level and let go of fear is to tell someone about your fear. Often the result is an immediate reduction in your fear. Talking about your fear is like opening the basement door and letting out the fearsome, barking dogs below. Although the sound may be terrifying when you cannot see the cause of it, just opening up the door and letting the cause of the terror emerge into daylight has the immediate effect of taking away its power to frighten. Suddenly, you see that they are just dogs wagging their tails, demanding food and a walk outside.

The two best resources for seeking help outside of yourself are:

1. Talking to a friend or family member—Remember to find someone you can trust to actually listen. It is important that you can simply express your fear without interruption, correction, helpful advice, and judgment. Once you have expressed your fear, let your own words reverberate in your ear so that you can hear yourself. If you can hear yourself, you will be able to assess the reality of your situation much more objectively than when you were worrying about it silently. With a more objective take on the fear, you can assess the cause and the possible steps you can take to solve the problem.
2. Working with a professional counselor—Sometimes, for very good reasons, you may not want to reveal your fears to someone you know. Or you may have already tried to talk out your fears without success. Or the cause of your fears may be too deep or hidden for you to deal with yourself. If you have unconscious saboteurs at work, you will find that normal strategies to let go of your fears do not help. This is the time to work with a professional to uncover the source of your fears or your inability to let them go. Find a professional counselor who has a track record of getting rapidly to the root of a problem and resolving it equally rapidly, rather than commit you to long-term therapy with no end in sight.

## CONCLUSION

I have worked with a fair number of traders who were overwhelmed with fear and anxiety. Regardless of how their problems with fear began, over time they all begin to experience the same kind of consequences: Loss of concentration and focus, inability to follow their trading rules, increased losses in the markets, deterioration of physical well-being, loss of self-discipline, problems with their important relationships. The list goes on and on.

The good news is that there is a strategy that can quickly and effectively reduce your fears and allow you to just let them go. The first step of the strategy begins with taking action; small, easy actions that can immediately affect the source of the fear will empower you and instantly reduce your level of fear. The second step builds on the first by introducing rewards that make you want to take action. The third step helps you to let go by clearing your mind of fear through meditative practice. And the final step gives you a safety valve for your feelings by allowing you to release them safely to a caring listener or a trained counselor who can help you to get at the root of your fears. In a world in which fear comes at a trader from every corner, it is essential that he or she let go of fear before fear takes control of the wheel.

---

*Resentment is an emotion that you get to keep when you do not forgive yourself for why you took the feeling on in the first place.*

---

CHAPTER 10

# Letting Go of Resentment

If there is one thing that each of us shares with traders, it is the need to handle negative emotions so that they do not sabotage our life. In an average workday, a trader often has to deal with the roller coaster ride of emotions as a trade goes wildly in the wrong direction and then wildly in the right one—or vice versa. Greed, fear, shame, regret, anger, and anticipation. . .all these emotions come on without warning. Great traders experience them along with struggling traders. The difference is how they handle them.

## HANDLING TOXIC EMOTIONS

One of the most toxic of all emotions is resentment. Often, resentment occurs as a result of a loss and loss is the name of the game for traders. If a trader feels responsible for the loss, he will not feel resentment. But, if he feels that he is not responsible for the loss, resentment will often follow. For traders, losses can occur for reasons that are beyond their control, that is, they are the result of actions by others that are unethical, irresponsible, predatory, careless, and thoughtless, or purely accidental. For example:

- A trader may have lost a great deal of money in the market because his trading was suddenly interrupted by a person who should have known better, such as a spouse who demanded his attention for a trivial reason.

- Or he may have experienced losses created by a market that was artificially manipulated by an individual or group that reaped great rewards for themselves while incurring terrible losses for innocent investors and traders.
- Or a trader may have entered into a partnership with one or more traders who feathered their nest(s) at his expense or misrepresented their situation or made bad business decisions that cost him dearly.
- Or a trader may have purchased a trading system that came with guarantees or inflated results or misrepresentations, only to discover its problems, with no recourse, too late and after too much loss.
- Or a trader may have used a business service, such as an accountant or computer support company, which provided such bad service that it resulted in losses in his trading business.

Any one of a long list of experiences in a trader's day can result in a loss of his focus and productivity. Some of these experiences are so small that they quickly roll off his skin; but others may result in serious and/or permanent changes. The resulting costs to the trader can breed resentment, which can eat away at his insides, diverting his focus, and draining his energies.

## A LESSON IN LETTING GO

When the plane carrying NBC Sports chairman Dick Ebersol and his two sons crashed, the older son was able to drag his father from the burning plane, but the younger son perished. It appeared as though the crash was caused by human error compounded by bad weather. However, when asked about her feelings about the tragedy, the boy's mother, television actress Susan St. James, explained that she had always told her children to live by the following axiom:

> *"Feeling resentment is like taking poison to kill the person who wronged you."*

This brave mother had instantaneously let go of any bitterness she could have legitimately felt for the pilots or air-traffic controller or airplane manufacturer. Instead of bearing resentment for the death of her younger son, without losing a beat, she had moved on to gratitude for the survival of her husband and older son. She chose to cherish the memories of her lost son and do whatever she could to make the best of a dreadful loss. Yes, she still feels the pain of the loss and, yes, she will grieve for her son for a long time. But, she will not be trapped in the toxic world of resentment that will prevent her from being wife and mother to the rest of her family.

## MAKING THE DECISION

There is a lot to be learned by traders from this story. Letting go of any resentment allows a person with a terrible loss to move on to a new life, to future happiness and success. Rather than being stuck in a destructive emotional loop that simply consumes you with each new cycle, the act of letting go allows you to drop all the emotional baggage in a single act. But, how do you do such a simple, yet difficult thing when you have paid a terrible price for the actions of others?

Looking at the process of letting go from the end instead of the beginning, the last step in letting go of resentment is the decision to do so. That decision comes from an attitude. And that attitude comes from a philosophy, which is based on your beliefs. You cannot simply make the decision to let go of resentment. That decision, in order to motivate you to follow through on it, must be based on something stronger than the desire not to feel a certain way. Depending upon what you say to yourself about life and what it means to you, you will find it easy or hard to make that decision, and then to stick to it.

## CHECKING OUT YOUR BELIEFS

If the process of letting go starts with your beliefs, can't you simply add the right beliefs and just roll with the emotional punches instead of resisting? Well, yes and no. You need the right set of attitudes and ways of looking at the world that allow you to let go of bitterness, but adding them to your consciousness is not as simple as deciding it is better to forgive and go onward than to fight for justice and hold on to your righteous anger.

If you are holding on to a great deal of resentment in your life, you may have deeply held beliefs about life that come from early loss, betrayal, and wounding that never healed. These early and painful experiences often need professional counseling and therapy to heal. In this case, the only way to change your resentment-creating beliefs is to seek out help.

If your resentment response is not a chronic problem in your life that requires professional therapy, there are steps you can take on your own to make changes in your belief system. However, these steps require you to make a true commitment to change and will require you to do some hard inner work.

## Step One

The first step is to take a tough and honest look at your current beliefs. A belief is any statement that you make that is true for you. A good way to do this is to write out your answers to the following questions as truthfully as you can. This list is only a starting place for you, and you can add your own statements about life to this list.

- People are basically (good, bad, or neither). Explain why you think so.
- My life is (good, okay, or bad). Explain.
- You can count on the people you care about to (support you, to betray you, to forget you, to be there for you no matter what, etc.). Explain.
- No matter what I do, I (never fail, always fail, just miss the boat, just manage to make it through, etc.). Explain.
- The most important people in my life have been (great role models, flawed but basically good people, well-intentioned but destructive, evil and heartless, etc.). Explain.
- I expect that the rest of my life will be (happy and successful, full of struggle and periodic success, full of disappointment and loss, etc.). Explain.
- Accidents (do happen, occasionally happen, never happen—it's always someone's fault). Explain.
- The best way to handle a loss is to (experience it and then let it go, to resist it and to find a way to avoid dealing with it, fight it and seek justice and/or revenge). Explain.
- The world is (a good place full of opportunities, an evil place, full of accidents waiting to happen). Explain.

## Step Two

Now take a look at what you have written. Is it true? Is it what you really believe and feel? If not, what are you hiding from yourself? What is your true feeling about life?

## Step Three

For each question, ask yourself how your life has turned out based upon that particular belief. How will it continue in the future? If the results are non-productive, list them. For example, if you feel that people are basically bad, has this resulted in a lack of trust, a lack of closeness, or a well of criticism? Have these feelings produced positive relationships and professional success for you?

### Step Four

If you believed and felt differently, how would your life have turned out? What would your future look like? Close your eyes and imagine how it would be. The act of imagining is the most important step in this entire process. The more intensely you imagine feeling a particular way and then having a different outcome in your life, the more real it becomes. If you can use all of your senses to create a clear picture, and feel a deep feeling, and then describe it to yourself in words, this picture of the world will begin to replace the one you have put there.

### Step Five

Repeat step four every day for a month. When you awaken in the morning before you open your eyes, once again create the picture of your new view of the world, crank up those new feelings, and again describe the meaning of it to yourself.

New attitudes can occur rapidly when you feel the sting of the old ones and can see the great benefit of the new ones. If these new attitudes are reinforced by new experiences that bring positive results, they will become more and more influential in your thinking.

For example, if you decide that people who cut you off in traffic are inconsiderate fools who are ready to cause you an accident, you will feel anger the entire time you are driving on the city streets and crowded highways. Or do you believe that people who cut you off are so deeply anxious, unhappy, or full of emotion that they are unaware of what is happening around them and mean no one any harm. Once you start to think this way, you will feel empathy for the people who cut you off. You will wonder what is happening in their lives that is so consuming and you will stop feeling anger and frustration. Suddenly, you will get out of your car and no longer be emotionally exhausted. You may not even want that stiff drink you always pour yourself. Over time, your waist starts shrinking and you begin to sleep better. The benefits keep on coming.

## CONCLUSION

Resentment is one of the most toxic emotional states a trader can harbor, eating away at his good feelings and sapping his energy to be productive and successful. Since loss of any kind is fertile ground for resentment, a trader is more likely than most professionals to confront it. The best way to deal with this negative emotion is to simply let it go so that it rolls off you like water. Resisting it only makes it persist and grow in its influence. But, letting go requires an attitude shift and that attitude shift requires a commitment to examining your true beliefs and replacing them with life enhancing ones.

---

*Greed is fear of not getting the most of something. Give up the greed and you give up the fear, which will allow you to have what you deserve and perhaps even more.*

---

CHAPTER 11

# The Greed Addiction

If you are a serious trader, revisiting the subject of greed cannot be done often enough. Just as the price of freedom is eternal vigilance, the price of success in trading is eternal vigilance against greed.

Greed is there to sabotage you each time you face the prospect of making money in the markets. As the great confounder of judgment and destroyer of discipline, greed can cause you to hold a position long after the profits should have been taken or the losses cut. Like all great thieves, greed is an excellent sneak. It is subtle, wily, and hard to detect until it has its grip on you. Like the flu, you need to be regularly inoculated against greed since no one is immune and some individuals are particularly susceptible to it, and like the flu, no matter how many times you fall victim, you can catch it again in its new, mutated form.

## THE PERPETUALLY UNDONE TRADER

Roy, a brilliant man and a very poor trader, is the poster boy for a fatal case of greeditis. His trading systems are so dazzling with genius that it is difficult to imagine anyone using them without making millions. When Roy starts trading, he calls with the news that he is making money at the rate of some amazing percentage—as much as 100 percent per week. His astounding success will go on for seven or eight weeks during which he will call with plans for what he will do with all of his future earnings. As weeks pass, his plans become more and more elaborate and inflated as he dreams of great riches. Suddenly, the calls stop and he will not be heard from for a month or more during which time he has once again lost everything.

Why does a trader continue to lose all that he makes in the markets when his talent is as great or greater than the best traders in the field? In Roy's case, he is perpetually undone by his unbridled greed. Strangely enough, when Roy is poor, he is the least greedy individual you will ever meet. He would happily give you the shirt from his back. When he has no prospects of having any money, he will share whatever he has. However, just give him the vision of riches in the future, and Roy rapidly loses all sense of proportion, reality, and self-discipline. He breaks all of his own, most cherished trading rules until there is nothing left to trade.

It would be possible to make the case that traders like Roy are simply afraid of success or that they feel unworthy of success. However, nothing could be further from the truth in Roy's case. Roy loves success and believes deeply that he is worthy of it. In fact, he has powerful motivating images of himself in successful situations. Without these powerful unconscious motivators, Roy would never have achieved the level of success in other fields that he has already achieved.

The problem is that Roy becomes possessed by greed. It overtakes him with such power that he is unaware of its hold and he is helpless to fight it until it has taken everything back. Despite all of his best intentions, Roy is susceptible to greed's infectious power to sidetrack his success.

## THE BIOLOGY OF GREED

According to the dictionary, greed is "an overwhelming desire to have more of something such as money than is actually needed." But what does that really mean for a trader? Is greed simply an emotion like joy, desire, grief, or anger? Does it have more of an influence on us than just a transitory feeling or desire?

Although there is no available research on the biochemistry of greed, it is clear that greed has the power to send a chemical rush through us that compels us to put aside our common sense, our self-control, and our humanity. If other powerful emotional states create changes in our brains and our bodies, there is compelling evidence in the behavior surrounding greed to suggest that it does so as well.

### "A Hit of Greed, Anyone?"

Most of us know traders, friends, and even members of our own family who are so highly susceptible to addictions that they smoke, drink, gamble, take drugs, or eat excessively to the point of self-destruction. These people are unable to stop. It is also possible that the addicted person will be the one who looks back at us in the mirror every morning.

Studies have shown that people who are addicted to one thing are likely to be addicted to any or all of the other possible addictive substances. Often, highly addicted individuals can lead successful lives if their addictions can be controlled or if they were persuaded by reason or circumstance to avoid contact with addictive substances when they were young. However, once they succumb to the temptation of an addictive substance or behavior, they are often swept away by it.

### The Bottom Line

From what we know about addictions, it is not unreasonable to make the educated assumption that traders who enter the business for the excitement are in need of that hit or the emotional high to feel alive. These traders are addicted to the release of the brain chemicals that makes them feel happy or relaxed or euphoric. These same traders are vulnerable to all possible addictions. Then, one day, they suddenly encounter their first opportunity to achieve their first big score in the markets. Once they see and feel the possibility of making a killing in the markets, they suddenly begin to experience a rush of euphoria. As soon as they sample the powerful emotional high that comes with that first hit of greed, they are hooked.

### Can the Greed Addiction Actually Be Good for Your Trading?

Sometimes in the short run, a self-destructive behavior or pattern can produce positive results making it even more addictive. However, the only predictable long-term result for any addiction is woe, short and simple.

### The Antidote

Is there an antidote to the greed addiction? For some, like Roy our perennial loser, the antidote to the greed addiction is total loss. Without the prospect of making money, his addiction is under control. If you know that you are a greed junkie, here is a list of seven possible antidotes:

1. Stop or limit your trading. Limiting the amount of trading that you do can cut down on your exposure to the addictive cycle.
2. Make note of the pictures that you create when you are heading toward the addictive state of greed and change the pictures to snap you back into a normal state.

3. Cut back or stop the use of addictive substances and behaviors, all of which contribute to the likelihood of your being overcome by any other addiction. This would include cigarettes, alcohol, drugs, gambling, overeating, and so on. Clearly, this is a very difficult step and requires tremendous commitment and effort. The best way to go about this is to seek a support system. For example, join Alcoholics Anonymous or any other support group, or seek out a therapist or counselor.
4. Build a set of controls into your trading that limits your exposure to the hands-on decision to enter or exit a position. Examples would be established stop-loss orders or a third-party trader to run your system for you.
5. Relaxation techniques. Meditation is a very important factor in reducing the effect of addictions, because it turns the fight or flight mechanism off for 12 hours. This makes it very difficult for your brain to be over-stimulated by anything.
6. Exercise and proper nutrition. Like meditation, exercise appears to help to reduce or moderate addictive behaviors. For example, continuous exercise for an hour results in doubling serotonin production. A diet that is rich in B vitamins, fresh fruits, vegetables, and good proteins plus supplements is also extremely helpful. Cutting out the white foods (white flour, white sugar, white rice, white potatoes) has had anecdotal success in taming the addiction beast.
7. Find a coach, counselor, or friend. Like all addictions, greed must be addressed and cannot be ignored. It is best to find some form of outside support in working your way through it.

## CONCLUSION

Greed is the out-of-control beast that can chase away profits. If you are a trader who loves excitement and needs a daily fix of nicotine, caffeine, alcohol, or other stimulating drugs to get through the day, the chances are that greed is also one of your addictions of choice. A wise trader is one who recognizes the addictive power that greed can have over him and finds ways to avoid the temptation altogether or at the least to reduce its frequency and effect.

*When you are putting up your shield, you will not allow opportunity to come through.*

CHAPTER 12

# The Defensive Trader

Sid had a problem with his trading that was causing him to lose money. Instead of waiting for the buy signal from his system, Sid would anticipate the signal and buy too soon. If the trade took a slight tick downward after it was initiated, he would panic and sell. As soon as he sold, the market would resume its upward trend and his signal to buy would appear.

When asked about the cause of the problem, Sid vigorously denied that there was a problem with his trading performance. He blamed his losses on the system he had purchased and the volatility of the market that he followed. In Sid's mind, he had done everything correctly given the circumstances. For Sid, change was going to be impossible because he had taken a defensive position.

## IT'S NOT LUCK

Recently, I read a book used in an MBA course on leadership in business. In one study, the authors concluded that almost no difference existed between executives who rose to the top of their fields and those who dropped out along the way. These individual managers were equally intelligent, capable, productive, affable, committed, and ambitious. In some cases, regardless of the individual's efforts, it seemed that luck determined who was rewarded and who was not. Even discounting luck, the researchers found a single trait that characterized the not-so-lucky executives: They were defensive.

What does it mean to be defensive? A defensive trader is one who finds it difficult to take direction, correction, advice, or constructive criticism. The individual may get upset and angry, but it is more than likely that he will simply explain and justify his behavior with rationalizations, excuses, and reasons. What he cannot do is say, "I am wrong and need to make a correction."

For a trader, the problem with being defensive is that nothing can change if the present course is always defended, even though it is moving the trader in the wrong direction.

## NOT LISTENING

A friend who sits on the board of directors of a private organization had a serious problem with a consultant that had been hired to manage its public relations. When the members of the board tried to tell the consultant what they wanted, she always took a defensive posture. Frustrated and angry, the board eventually elected to fire her. Their chief complaint was that she spent all of her time defending her position and not listening to their concerns. What they wanted her to do was to acknowledge their concerns. Instead, she simply defended the status quo so that nothing could be done to correct the problems presented by the board.

As a defensive trader, you will soon find yourself in a position comparable to the defensive manager and the public relations consultant. If you are not listening and are unable to acknowledge a problem, you can expect the following consequences in your professional and personal life:

- **Your most important relationships will suffer.** The people you work and live with need to be able to tell you when something is wrong or if something is bothering them. If they cannot get you to hear them because you are defending the status quo, they will eventually stop trying. When they stop trying, they will shut you out. For a trader, the vital lines of communication and support will wither and die.

  When you admit that you have made a mistake or that you need to improve a situation, the people who brought you the problem will immediately stop their criticism, attack, or presentation. You have addressed the complaint and now everyone is on the same team. The words, "You are right!" mend fences, build support and team spirit, and lead to compromise.
- **Your trading will not improve.** No trader should consider himself incapable of learning or improving. To fail to improve means that you

will be lucky to maintain the status quo. Markets change. Traders need to be willing to adjust to these changes. If you are defensive, you will find it difficult to make the needed adjustments.

- **You will miss opportunities.** Defensive traders are poor listeners. Since your intellectual capital is spent on building defenses, you will not be tuned in to the opportunities buried in identifying a problem and finding a creative solution.
- **When you ARE right, no one will hear you.** If you have consistently taken a defensive position, no one will be willing to listen to you when you are actually right about a situation or a problem. Like the boy who cried, "Wolf!" too often, no one will believe you when a wolf does appear. So, being willing to admit that you are wrong can actually make your being right easier for others to accept.
- **You fail to mature.** It is difficult for a trader to grow in maturity and competence since you are constantly defending the status quo. Even if you hire a trader's coach, go to counseling, or take courses and seminars, you will find yourself needing to fortify the apparent chinks in your trading armor rather than redesigning it or mending it.
- **You are more vulnerable to loss, attack, and the vagaries of the markets and life.** If you read about the great battles in history, you will find many stories of generals who lost their armies because they failed to recognize their weaknesses for fear of appearing indecisive. Rather than admitting a weakness, they justified their position to the point of losing everything. Remember that defensiveness invites even more attacks, making you even more vulnerable.

## THE NEED TO DEFEND

There was a very good reason why Sid always found reasons for what he did. He had been raised in a very critical home environment. Regardless of what he did as a child, his mother and father always found something wrong with it. Sid was a very bright and competent child. Instead of praising him for his accomplishments, his parents found something in his achievements to criticize.

Sid awoke each morning with a sense of impending doom. What would his parents find wrong with him today? No matter what he tried, he could not make it through the day having pleased them. Even as an adult, his parents could not stop their criticism. When visiting them, he would often change his entire outfit two or three times until he was absolutely certain it would not generate criticism. However, he was always wrong about that, too.

Sid's only path to survival in an environment like this was to learn self-defense. He quite naturally fell into a pattern of defending himself that followed him throughout his life. The minute he perceived that he was under attack, he immediately began to formulate a defense strategy. The fact that these "attacks" were constructive or even necessary advice did not register with Sid's unconscious mind, which was hypersensitive to the faintest whiff of an attack.

Most people do not grow up in homes as critical as Sid's. However, many people come from homes with varying levels of criticism and judgment. If it does not come from their homes, it very often comes from their peers. From my observation of the traders who come for coaching, the most critical homes are often the ones where the parents are highly intelligent and well educated. These parents expect near-perfection from their children and are not satisfied with anything less. The result for their children is the need to be on the defensive about their performance in every aspect of their lives.

## A WAY OUT OF DEFENSIVENESS

For Sid, the way out of defensiveness was to build his sense of self-esteem. At the heart of defensiveness is a sense of unworthiness and powerlessness. A trader who feels good about himself and has a secure sense of his own worthiness will not fear making a mistake and owning up to it publicly.

As a first step in his recovery, we worked on building Sid's awareness of how he came to be so defensive as a powerless child. When he began to understand why he had needed to defend himself against the steady stream of criticism, he began to dismantle his defense systems because he was no longer a powerless child but a strong and independent adult.

Next, we focused on the things that Sid did well and on all of his achievements. We went back through his childhood and celebrated all of his un-acknowledged achievements. He listed his strengths and the things that he did right. Then, he learned how to visualize himself performing well and being acknowledged for his achievements.

The final step of his recovery was rehearsing his acceptance of criticism, correction, blame, and attacks. Some of the criticism was constructive and some was negative. It did not matter in the rehearsals. Sid needed to understand that all criticism and correction should be acknowledged. People who are willing to speak their minds about what they perceive as wrong need to know that they have been heard. Otherwise, they simply get angry, frustrated, and willing to take action that you do not want to face.

Here are the nine steps in responding to correction, advice, criticism, and attack that Sid learned:

1. Listen carefully without fear. Remember that the speaker is taking a risk in being open and honest about a perceived problem.
2. Paraphrase back to the speaker's satisfaction what you believe he or she is trying to tell you.
3. Ask for confirmation that you have properly understood what the speaker has said.
4. If there is a problem inherent in your performance, acknowledge it without excuses, reasons, or justifications. At this point, it does not matter if you are being wrongly accused. You need to own up to your part in the matter and only your part as they see it. Realize that it is their opinion but that it may have value for you. Gems of good information may be missed if you block people from expressing their opinion. Even one piece of advice can make all the difference in your performance.
5. Work toward a mutually agreed upon solution. Ask for potential solutions and advice.
6. Make a commitment to work on the solution.
7. Thank the speaker for being willing to bring the problem to light and for his help in solving it. Once you have taken this conciliatory step, all of the potential negative feelings that were in the speaker will have been neutralized. He will have no reason left to feel that you are in the wrong, that you have not been listening, and that you will not cooperate in correcting the problem. You are now part of the solution.
8. Follow up and follow through. Once you have agreed upon a solution, work on the solution and keep updating the speaker on your progress. This follow up is not only critical in solving the problem, but in building a stronger sense of teamwork.
9. Reward yourself each time you make it through a situation in which the feedback is negative without resorting to defensiveness.

The purpose of this rehearsal is to make you comfortable with the process of responding to correction, criticism, blame, or attack and automatically responding with a strategy of strength. If you do not have anyone to rehearse with, shut yourself in a room and rehearse out loud or mentally rehearse different scenarios until you feel prepared to not respond defensively.

## CONCLUSION

In the business world, the single thread that connects highly talented people who fail to achieve their potential is defensiveness. A defensive trader is at an equal disadvantage in his professional life. Defensiveness prevents a trader from hearing the important feedback that he needs to improve his performance, his relationships, and his business. It stands between him and the flexibility he needs to adapt to the perpetually changing markets and it prevents him from growing. A trader's defensiveness makes him vulnerable and builds a wall around him that isolates him from opening himself up to positive changes.

If a trader came from a critical and judgmental environment, he learned early in life to become defensive as soon as the feedback sounded challenging. That automatic defensiveness comes from insecurity, a sense of powerlessness, and feelings of unworthiness. A defensive trader can become a team player that responds to problems with confidence and a demonstrated willingness to listen, acknowledge, and to solve the problem. The process for unlearning defensiveness requires courage, commitment, and perhaps some outside help, but the result will be a strong and successful trader with the social skills to succeed.

---

*Feeling bad has the same thrust as feeling good but with a negative outcome. What is your choice?*

---

CHAPTER 13

# Transformation of Feelings

Are you one of the many traders who think that feelings have nothing to do with making money in the markets? If so, then you are also one of the many traders whose success in trading is held captive by his feelings.

The most successful traders in the industry are consistent traders. But, in order for a trader to be consistently successful in the markets, he needs to follow predetermined rules that he believes will give him a positive outcome. The problem for most traders, however, is that the ability to follow those rules depends upon a set of feelings that keep him disciplined. For a trader who wants to build a long and consistently successful career, these positive feelings are as valuable as having tomorrow's market results in your hands today.

If self-sabotage does not come between a trader and following his rules, he will create a comfortable feeling that will support his efforts. But if, in the process of becoming a trade he loses money consistently, experiences a large loss, or is inconsistent in his results, he will develop a negative conditioning with associated negative feelings about the choices he makes.

## FEELINGS THAT CREATE REALITY

For all of us, feelings are the final element in the process of how we create our reality. First comes the experience; next, we tell ourselves the story about the experience; and then comes the feeling(s) associated with the story. As a result of the repetition of the story over time, with the associated feelings, we will create a reality that reflects those feelings. For example, pain that is associated with a loss in the markets will eventually create more and more loss by impairing judgment, preventing a trader from following his rules, preventing him from pulling the trigger, and holding him back from taking necessary risk.

However, when there is a conditioning for negative feelings, an immediate response can occur without the story that was originally attached to the bad feeling. For example, the story of the original and painful loss may be forgotten, but the feelings of pain and fear may rise to the surface each time a trader attempts to enter a trade. To let go of these negative and sabotaging feelings, you must change the original story, or change the feelings attached to the story.

By understanding the process of your "creating reality strategy," you will begin to understand where changes must take place in order to transform the conditioning.

## THE TYPICAL STRATEGY FOR CREATING REALITY

Humans first take in information from their five senses based on the story they create about that information. When we experience an event, we store the experience based on what we heard, saw, smelled, touched, and even tasted. The more of these sensory details we store and remember from that experience, the more significant these stories become for us and the more real they become in our minds. The most significant stories eventually will create a conditioned response. Thus, if we are in an accident while driving and we continue to relive the experience in our minds—hear the sounds of the crash, feel the pain, smell the smoke from the fire, see that truck careening toward us, and even taste the blood from our injury, we will have an experience that will continue to have a profound influence over our lives long after it occurred.

### Filtering Stories

Life experiences condition you in the way you will filter the original experience of the story. Either a significant person in your life told you how to interpret this story, or you have developed an opinion about the story. These influences create a reality filter for you that only lets in the information that you already believe to be true. When you have a positive experience, your filter will make you anticipate the same positive experience you had in the past. The reverse is true for negative experiences.

## Sensation/Feeling

If the experience of an original story had a positive outcome, you will have a pleasant sensation or feeling in your body. Our body interprets a good feeling as a healthy experience. If the feeling is uncomfortable, we constrict or restrict our bodily functions and create disease in our body. We then learn that negative feelings should be avoided because they are associated with physical or emotional pain. In the case of someone who trades in the financial markets, negative feelings associated with a drawdown will very often lead to sabotaging future trades. Traders avoid negative feelings even if they believe that they will earn money from the overall system. Thus, the possibility of a loss becomes something to avoid.

"How do you feel?" asks the therapist as she assesses her client. Why is it important for the therapist to know this or more likely for her client to recognize it in himself? The therapist or coach wants to:

- Identify the issue that first connected her client to the problem he is trying to overcome.
- Know that her client is attached to the feelings of the original event, so she can dissipate those feelings with new associations.
- Insure that his stories are not so disassociated from the feeling that they are just stories. This disconnect happens when it is too painful psychologically to feel the feeling that was first attached to the story.
- Discover when he has felt similar feelings before in his life. Since he is likely to have a chain of events attached to the current loss, she will be able to assist him in defusing all of those events.
- Redirect the negative feeling into a positive or neutral association with the original event, so he will be able take action from logic, not from negative feelings.

Andy had a chain of events in his life that kept him from following his rules. The psychological term used is *Gestalt.* From childhood, Andy felt he was not worthy of achieving great success. His father repeatedly told him that this was true and little Andy believed his father. As a result, he learned to play the character of the unworthy individual and sabotaged his efforts to be a winner in anything he tried to accomplish, whether it was in his personal life or in his professional life. For example:

- In baseball, he always managed to be just an average player even though when he was in practice he was clearly the most talented player.
- He managed to lose his front-runner position for student council by getting sick.

- He lost the young woman who was attracted to him by saying something stupid and inappropriate.

With a minor in psychology, Andy realized the Gestalt was keeping him from his best efforts. But understanding the problem did not stop the curse. He began his career in finance in the back office, providing support to professional traders. Soon, he dreamed of becoming a trader himself. Eventually, he had positioned himself to be considered by his firm to risk financing him as a trader.

Andy's first drawdown resurrected the old Gestalt. Fortunately, he now had the psychological background to understand what was happening. He quickly hired a therapist who asked him to run through his series of negative stories. "How do you feel about it?" After years of retelling these stories, Andy no longer had feelings attached to them, except the drawdown experience. But, as a "good patient," he produced the appropriate feeling that he no longer felt. Fortunately, his therapist recognized the emotional disconnection. Through hypnosis, the feelings flowed from the most recent event all the way back to the root cause: His father telling Andy that he was not worthy of achieving success.

When Andy confronted his father about the negative messages in his childhood, his father told Andy that he had feared that he would not be able to send his son to college. To protect Andy from being disappointed by not having a bright future, his father had told him that he was not worthy of achieving great success. Rather than wanting his son to fail, he very much wanted him to enjoy a successful life.

## Blocking Feelings

I like to think of feelings as being the final frontier in mastering any goal. Feelings complete the circuitry in the natural current of energy, events, and intentions that flow as a person processes his life. In that process, we learn to create the passion necessary to ignite our senses, to recognize opportunity, to create innovative ideas, and to learn valued lessons. Unfortunately, well-intended people teach us to block our feelings. Blocked feelings can result from any number of experiences such as:

- Parents who say, "You're a big boy—big boys don't cry."
- Sports coaches who say, "Act like a man."
- Business professionals who let you know that it is "not professional" to show your negative emotions.
- And in the case of traders—those trading mentors who say "keep emotions out of trading."

Blocked negative emotions will inevitably find an outlet for their expression, just like steam will find an outlet or explode from its confines when the pressure builds too high. Often those situations caused by blocked emotions will look and feel familiar; and they will be repeated again and again until the underlying wound that causes them is healed. When you ignore the warning signs and continue to repress those feelings, they will lead to negative physical manifestations such as physical illness.

## WINNING ON A LOSING PATH

Amir was one of those traders who blocked his negative feelings. Eventually, he had a stroke that crippled his ability to earn money. He lost all of his assets, including his wife and children. Having neglected his family, he failed to accrue any emotional collateral with them. Although he had provided them with a comfortable life materially, he had lived his life like a bachelor, rarely participating in family activities. To those who knew him casually, Amir appeared to be a happy person. But, those closest to him would describe him as a very intense man.

Amir learned to repress negative feelings early. His father pushed him away as a child when he was crying and told Amir's mother that she was not allowed to comfort him. Later, Amir witnessed the brutal murder of his father by someone who did not agree with his religious beliefs. Remembering what his father taught him, Amir did not shed a tear. When his mother could not support all three of her children, she sent Amir to live with his uncle in the United States. After graduating from college, Amir worked in his uncle's factory. Then, a family friend who managed a hedge fund introduced him to trading.

In his professional life, Amir continued to be an expert at blocking negative feelings. This enabled him to follow the trading rules his friend taught him without experiencing negative feelings when the system went into a drawdown. And while he was successful, initially, as a money-making trader, his blocked feelings eventually toppled his world.

## HOW DO YOU DEAL WITH NEGATIVE FEELINGS?

### Strategy #1

From the examples described above, ignoring and surpressing negative feelings does not produce good, long-term results. The following five steps are how many therapists or coaches train their clients to handle negative emotions:

1. Acknowledge that these feelings exist.
2. Notice where (specifically) you feel stresses and tensions in your body.
3. Transform (change) the submodalities (the details of the story that are driving the emotions.) For example in Andy's case: "My father wants me to be successful." Then, follow with a detailed story that involves the truth about this new story.
4. Transform the submodalities of the emotions themselves. For example: Notice what you feel and where you are feeling it and ask yourself to remember what it was like to have good feelings in those areas of your body.
5. Notice specifically how the sensations or the submodalities change or dissipate their intensity until the feeling is no longer a crippling issue.

Although this appears to be a simple process, most people find it difficult to accomplish without the assistance of a therapist or coach who is trained to facilitate this model.

### Strategy #2

This second way of dealing with feelings is one that a trader can do on his own. Follow these five steps:

1. Acknowledge that the feeling exists.
2. Humanize that feeling and ask it this question: "What are you trying to tell me?"
3. If you get an answer, write it down. Study it. Now, make a commitment to do something to change your behavior so that your behavior does not have to give you uncomfortable sensations in order to get your attention.

   For example, the answer you receive could be:

   - You are overworked and need a vacation. Solution: Commit to taking a vacation.
   - You are stressing yourself and need to choose to do activities that will de-stress you. Solution: Commit to taking a walk after work, or going to the gym, or meditating each morning.
   - You need help because you cannot change these feeling by yourself. Solution: Commit to setting up an appointment with a counselor or a coach.

4. If you do not get an answer at first, then ask that humanized feeling to reveal the answer as soon as it feels you are ready to listen.
5. As soon as you get an answer, you must follow through on the message or you will continue to sabotage your efforts with negative feelings. If you do not get an answer and the negative feeling persists, then you need help from a trained professional.

## CONCLUSION

In trading, feelings are an essential element in the decision-making process; however, negative sensations will produce sabotaged actions and create losses. Negative feelings create negative conditioning. Unless you change the negative conditioning that prevents you from following your rules, that conditioning will only grow stronger. Only positive feelings and the positive conditioning they create will allow you to follow your trading rules consistently. By following the two strategies outlined in this article, you can begin to transform this old conditioning into positive feelings that support your trading, rather than sabotaging it.

---

*In your mind's eye, overlay a picture of what would be the ideal of a negative situation until the negative picture becomes unreal.*

---

CHAPTER 14

# Comfort in Pain

This story was related to me recently by a trader named Joe.

> *"Success makes me uncomfortable. For years I've been telling my family and myself that my life goal is to be a successful trader. But, the truth is that the moment I get too close to my goal, I sabotage my trading so that I can feel comfortable again. And the part that scares me the most is that the pain does not put me off. In fact, if I were to be completely honest, I'd have to say that I feel comfort in the pain."*

If Joe were the only trader who found comfort in pain, it would be an interesting anecdote. However, far too many traders feel the same internal conflict that Joe feels as soon as he begins to approach the feelings of fulfillment and satisfaction. Suddenly, he is drawn to the darker side of his life, the place that feels right to him.

One of the most powerful foes a trader must face is his own comfort in pain. What feels comfortable and secure can also be the one thing a trader must avoid. Since the natural human tendency is to go toward comfort and away from discomfort, this attraction to the feeling of pain presents a trader with a great conflict: Should he be uncomfortable by avoiding the thing (pain) that makes him feel comfort or should he feel comfort by adhering to the thing that brings him pain?

## THE SOURCE

As Mr. Spock, the half-Vulcan/half-human First Officer on the starship Enterprise, would say, it is not logical that an individual would choose pain over more positive experiences. However, this choice has nothing to do with logic. It also has nothing to do with conscious choice. Joe's own story is an all-too-familiar one. Having been raised by highly critical and rejecting parents, Joe was accustomed to the feelings of emotional pain. Anxious to please his parents, Joe's efforts were continually met with ridicule and a lack of appreciation. When Joe won the starring role in his high school play, his parents attended the performance, but afterward critiqued his efforts to the point of utter humiliation. His nearly straight-A report cards elicited complaints instead of praise. For Joe, no success brought the comfort of praise—only a sense of loss and pain. He summed up his experience this way:

> *"Pain is my comfort zone. It's that really familiar place with the hearth fire burning, the home cooking, and the ever-present sense of impending doom. It's the place I go to when I have a loss. It's the place I go to when my negative emotions are stirred. It's the place I both dread and find comfort in at the same time. My parents introduced me to this place as a child and even with them long gone, I find it impossible not to visit it when my life takes a turn for the worst."*

Like Joe, many high-achieving traders find themselves sabotaging their efforts to succeed in order to return to the place that feels the most comfortable to them. Drawn to the pain comfort zone, they create losses in order to feel that way once again. Pain for them has associations with parents, with childhood, and with times that may not have been so innocent. Feeling pain can bring Joe and other traders like him a sense of connection with people and places that are long gone but which hold a great emotional tug on their hearts. So, feeling pain can almost be like looking at an album of old pictures, or watching an old home movie, or smelling a pie baking in the oven that reminds you of your home and your childhood.

## THE LURE OF PAIN

The human brain is a three-pound chemical laboratory that creates chemical responses to various stimuli. In response to something pleasurable, we produce a set of chemicals in our brain that make us feel an intense and wonderful sensation. As a result, we want to feel that way again, and so we try to reproduce that pleasurable experience. In response to pain, we also produce a set of chemicals that produce another intense set of sensations that we normally would want to avoid ever feeling again.

So, if we are attracted to pleasure and repelled by pain, why would anyone then be drawn to pain? Not only can pain represent a familiar place that reminds one of childhood and memories long gone, pain has its own physiological/psychological appeal. As we experience pain, that same chemical reaction in our brain that floods us with intense feelings also makes us feel very much alive at the same time. While in the throes of this intense emotional and physical state, we also tend to blot out anything else that is happening at the same time.

Anyone who has lost a loved one through death knows that feeling of intense pain that drapes everything around you in a kind of misty gauze. You feel like you are on some kind of strange drug that simultaneously heightens and dulls your senses. You find yourself looking at the world from the outside, no longer part of what is happening, wondering at the foolishness of those around you who do not understand.

In this emotional and biochemical state of intense pain and loss, the world is a very intense and unreal place. But, it can also be a very appealing place for an individual who has difficulty feeling his own feelings. This state of intensity can actually become almost addictive. The fact that it is bio-chemically created adds to the credibility of this observation. Thus, I believe that a fair number of the traders who find comfort in pain are actually addicted to the intense feelings they experience when they are in pain. Those feelings not only feel comfortable and familiar, they also feel strangely pleasant and appealing.

## FINDING PAIN

For a trader to find comfort in pain is equivalent to sticking his own hand into the beehive. He is certain to get stung. The quickest way for him to go to that place is to create his own losses. A trader may feel that he simply goes to that comforting place whenever he feels pain or experiences a loss. However, unconsciously he is actually drawn to that place and will, therefore, create losses in order to experience the pain that brings him comfort.

Another way for a trader to enter the pain comfort zone is through the people, places, or times that he misses from his past. If those people who are the most dear to us are also tied to extreme pain and loss, we are likely to find a way to create trading losses in order to be close to those people we miss.

## MOVING INTO A BETTER NEIGHBORHOOD

If you are a trader who feels good in the pain comfort zone, you need to move into a better neighborhood—a comfort zone that allows you to feel good when things are actually good and not painful. But how?

When Joe described his pain comfort zone, he used words that would normally describe a warm, pleasant, and safe place:

- that really familiar place
- the hearth fire burning
- home cooking
- comfort
- my parents
- me as a child

These are the very same images that Joe has attached to the feelings of pain, thereby making the experience of pain a goal rather than something to avoid. Instead of associating pain with comfort, what Joe must do is to associate pain with pain and pleasure with pleasure. Once he makes this new association, he will then move into a new comfort zone, one that is actually comfortable with having achieved success rather than loss.

## STRATEGIES FOR MAKING A CHANGE

Neuro-linguistic programming (NLP) offers traders like Joe a very effective set of strategies for making a change in his patterns of behavior and thinking. This strategy will be easier and quicker with the help of a trained professional, but if a trader is committed to making the change and willing to do the work himself, it is entirely possible for him to make this transformation on his own. I worked with Joe on this process and here is what he did:

- The first step for Joe to take was to recognize that he had made deep, unconscious associations with pain that brought him comfort.
- The next step was difficult because Joe had to be willing to experience the pain he actually felt when his parents rejected him. In other words, he had to be willing to really experience the experience.

- Once he had felt the pain, he had to be willing to feel how uncomfortable it really was and conclude that he did not want to feel that way again.
- Then, in the midst of those intense feelings, he had to focus on something that brought him real joy, such as taking his son out to the park and playing catch with him on a sunny spring day.
- As he raised his feelings from pain to joy, he then intensified those feelings until they completely filled his being. At that point, he then began to picture himself succeeding in his trading, making winning trades, coming home to tell his wife and son about his success, and all the things they would then do with his success.
- Now that he had made his first new association of those feelings of joy with his trading success, he was instructed to repeat the new association over and over again each day for a full month. Each time he experienced the feelings of joy, he instantly transferred the intense feeling of joy to images of his trading successfully, of his winning trades, and of his happy life that results from his trading success.

It was essential in this process that Joe was willing to keep working at it until it felt perfectly natural. At first, it felt unreal and uncomfortable for him. After all, Joe had been associating pain with pleasure for a long time and his brain had a long history of accommodating this neural pathway until it was a deeply embedded groove. However, the good news is that Joe was committed to working his way out of his comfort in the pain zone, and he is now trading at an entirely new level of success. He loves feeling joy in his success and in building his new dream house for his family. Occasionally, he has a relapse, which is to be expected. However, when he does relapse, he calls me and we complete a visualization on the phone that allows him to jump back into his new comfort zone.

## CONCLUSION

Traders who have experienced pain in their childhood on a regular basis are at great risk for finding comfort in pain. This association of pain with comfort makes a trader far more likely to sabotage his trading in order to put him into his comfort zone. Any other loss or pain in his life will bring him into this zone and allow him to stay in it, unwilling to bring success into his life with the discomfort it would create in his world. The best way out of this negative situation for a trader is to either work on his own or with a trained professional to break the association he has with pain, making the experience of pain to be uncomfortable and linking success with comfort, instead. Once a trader has been able to make the change in his associations with pain, like Joe, he will discover that the world of successful trading truly opens up for him for the first time.

---

*Compliments feel good on both sides. What feeling do both sides have with complaints?*

---

CHAPTER 15

# Don't Complain

This simple piece of advice came from Benjamin Disraeli, arguably the most famous English statesman of the nineteenth century, and certainly the most colorful one: "Don't complain, don't explain."

Disraeli's recommendation could easily have been directed to traders today as an excellent means of increasing their profits. How? Just for starters, learning how to stop complaining and explaining will dramatically increase your sense of power and influence in your professional and personal life. A sense of personal power is vital to building self-confidence, which is one of the keys to making money in the markets.

## THE DON'T COMPLAIN PART

What does it mean to complain? When you complain, you are probably doing one of the following:

- expressing unhappiness
- verbalizing the fact that you are experiencing distress: pain, illness, loss, or emotional upset
- accusing someone of doing something distressing, illegal, or undesirable
- protesting something

What Disraeli meant about complaining, of course, will never be explained. But, from what I have seen of traders who do a lot of it, complaining rarely results in a successful professional and personal outcome for them. Why?

In short, when you complain you are expressing dissatisfaction with things the way they are. When you chronically complain, you are giving public expression to a private sense of powerlessness, victimhood, and passivity. Chronic complainers are saying, in effect, that they are not responsible for the conditions of their own happiness and wellbeing. Many chronic complainers have never stopped feeling, unconsciously, that they are still children who are waiting for their parents or any responsible adult to take care of them and to correct their problems. Unfortunately, this is not an uncommon feeling.

## THE WHINER TRADER

Mark is a trader who came for consulting work with a long list of complaints about his trading, the markets, the industry service providers, his wife, his children, and life in general. Strangely, Mark had come from a stable and loving home, about which he should have had no complaints. And yet he did. His parents did not do enough for him. They should have given him a better education, a better neighborhood, a bigger allowance, and so on. The truth was that they had given him far too much. Mark had never been trained to see that he would have to provide for himself. Instead, his parents were always there to bail him out, to soothe his troubles away, and ease the pain of growing up. The result for Mark was the expectation that someone should be doing this for him the rest of his life. And when the universe did not solve all of his problems and meet all of his expectations, he complained. For Mark, complaining was a symptom of his failure to grow into an adult who was willing and able to take responsibility for himself, to meet his own needs, and to solve his own problems.

Helping Mark to understand what he needed to do was not easy and it required him to perform a lot of soul-searching. One of the most powerful moments in this process was when he listened to a tape of his interview with me. Listening to himself complaining about everything was painful for him because he had never heard himself in the role of "the great whiner." When Mark began to reduce his complaining to a reasonable level, both his professional and personal lives began to improve dramatically.

In stark contrast to Mark is another trader, Edward. Born to a heroin-addicted mother and an unknown father, Edward was placed in foster care at the age of six months. After three years, his grandparents finally located him and gained legal custody, rescuing him from a life of poverty and insecurity. These wonderful people raised him from that time onward in a nurturing environment in which they set reasonable limits and expectations.

As an adult, Edward is grateful for everything and complains about nothing. He is respectful and loving toward the grandparents who raised him. Instead of expecting them to educate him, he joined the military to pay for his college and graduate school degrees. He feels totally responsible for his life and is willing to do whatever it takes to reach his goals.

The postscript to this story is that a deprived early life does not mean that you simply walk away with a sense of gratitude and personal responsibility. Edward also bears scars and suffers from depression and low self-esteem. He merely has a different set of challenges to overcome. But, he has the great strength that comes from the willingness to take responsibility and not complain.

## THE HIGH COST OF COMPLAINING

One of the costs of complaining is that people do not want to be around you. Among the many reasons for this fact are:

- It is tedious to listen to someone complaining. (Unspoken Response: Who wants to be bored?)
- Complaining brings down the emotional temperature of a social gathering. (Unspoken Response: Who wants to have a bad time just when you were having such a good one?)
- Complainers seem weak and powerless. (Unspoken Response: Who wants to be around someone like that?)
- Complaints remind everyone else about a problem they are trying to solve on their own or avoid, if possible. (Unspoken Response: Who wants to be anxious all over again?)
- Complainers appear to be pessimistic, with the underlying assumption that things are always bad and hopeless. (Unspoken Response: Who needs that message?)
- Complainers sometimes appear to have a hidden agenda, which is that they are actually asking the listener to take responsibility for fixing the problem. Or worse, they are actually blaming the listener for the problem. (Unspoken Response: Why would I want to fix your problem or take the blame for it? Get lost!)

Thus, you can measure the first cost of complaining by all of the people who do not want to spend time with you, listen to you, work with you, or depend upon you. The second great cost of complaining is the loss of your own self-esteem. If you are a chronic complainer, you have relinquished the sense of personal power that comes with taking responsibility for solving your problems and for your own feelings, happiness, and wellbeing. This loss of personal power leaves an individual feeling weak and victimized, with the result that he becomes angry and depressed and his sense of himself suffers.

## TURNING DOWN THE COMPLAINING VOLUME

Here are four effective strategies for gradually reducing the amount of complaining that you do.

### Strategy #1

Listening to yourself: One of the simplest ways to stop complaining is to listen to yourself talk. Actually listen without judging or attempting to censor. Many people think that they can will themselves to stop. However, just determining that you will complain less may actually make the situation worse. You will be focusing on what not to do. Your brain does not process the word "not" so much as it creates pictures of things for goal setting. Therefore, when you tell yourself not to think about that chocolate cake, all your brain hears is "chocolate cake," and you will simply be creating the image of it in your mind, thus making it even more real to you. When you listen to yourself as you talk, and you do it without any sense of judgment, you will actually hear what you are saying. Just like the great whining trader, Mark, who began to turn around his complaining after hearing a tape of his interview, you can create the same effect by simply listening to yourself talk.

### Strategy #2

Surround yourself with noncomplainers. Remember when your parents would say, "Birds of a feather flock together?" Well, sadly, they were right about that one. A good example of this principle was a trader I worked with three years ago. John changed firms from one at which everyone complained to another where complaining was considered bad form. Within a brief period, John's complaining had stopped completely. It is instructive to listen to the people in your personal and professional life. Have you surrounded yourself with complainers? Do they seem to play the one-upmanship game to see who has the most about which to complain? If so, you may want to find friends who are more positive and who have a sense of personal responsibility.

### Strategy #3

Keep a journal. Write down the things about which you find yourself complaining. After each complaint, write a strategy for either correcting the situation yourself or for dealing with it in a way that makes you feel empowered and not feeling like a victim. For example, if you are always complaining about the drivers on the road and what idiots they are, you could decide to leave five or ten minutes earlier so that you are never in a rush and will not need to care if you are behind a slow driver. Thus, you have taken responsibility for your situation and for your feelings.

### Strategy #4

Get help. Find a counselor who can help you to work out your feelings of powerlessness and anger. Sometimes, the fastest way to transform attitudes is through the feedback you get from the outside world. For that reason you may also consider joining Toastmasters because it is a wonderful way to build self-esteem.

**The Case for Transforming Complaining** Many years ago, I attended a three-day personal development program that required the 40 or 50 participants to live together at the development center for the entire two and a half days. One result of this close encounter with total strangers was, after the first night, a series of complaints to the program leader and suggestions about how to make the program better. Now, this program leader was a very skillful individual and each time he was presented with a complaint, he would listen very carefully, paraphrase back the complaint to the complainer's satisfaction, and agree that the problem did indeed exist and needed fixing. Then, he would strongly urge the complainer to take responsibility for solving the problem. In some cases, he would actually assign the participant the job of solving the problem within a specified period of time. Needless to say, the number of complaints dropped to nothing. In the meantime, the program improved, as participants were shamed into solving the problems about which they had complained.

What the able leader of this program had done was to combine three positive results:

1. He allowed us to hear ourselves as complainers—an experience that few of us had ever had—in a public venue. We also heard others complain and we could hear ourselves in their voices.

2. He allowed us to grow in personal responsibility by making us accountable for the things about which we complained.
3. He showed us how to transform complaining into positive action.

**Turning Whining into Accomplishment** Not all complaining needs to be moaning and whining. In fact, the right kind of complaining can bring about positive transformations when it targets problems that need to be corrected. Robert Kegan and Lisa Laskow Lahey spent 15 years studying the subject of complaining. In their book, *How the Way We Talk Can Change the Way We Work: Seven Languages for Transformation* (Jossey-Bass, 2000) they write about how complaints, if properly decoded, can be turned into the "language of commitment" and positive transformation.

The steps to turning complaining into positive tools for transformation start with deconstructing the complaint itself by asking some important questions:

- What exactly is the complaint?
- Is the complaint well founded? Is it real and needs to be corrected?
- Is the one who is complaining committed to correcting the situation?

To answer the first question, you need to be able to clearly state the problem. If you are complaining that your partner never listens to you, is the problem with your partner or your expectations and feelings about him/her or yourself? If your partner never listens and the result is problems in your trading business, then the problem is real. If the problem is real, are you committed to correcting it? If so, what are you willing to do and how will you know when it is corrected?

But, suppose you discover that your complaints are actually based on your feelings of powerlessness and disappointment and anger. What then? Are you simply a complainer who looks for things to kvetch about? Consider the fact that behind every complaint is an idea or a belief or a value that a person is committed to. Get to the heart of your feelings. What is the problem? Instead of thinking of yourself as a complainer, think of yourself as someone committed to something—a person who identifies a problem, is committed to improving the situation, and is a problem solver. Then, empowered with this understanding, you can return to our list of strategies and add the final one:

### Strategy #5

Take action to correct the problem. Start by developing a plan for solving or correcting or reducing the problems that are at the heart of your complaints. Now that you are seeing each of your complaints as a legitimate problem that needs resolving and that you are a person committed to doing so, you can begin the process of taking action to improve your life. Once you start on this path, you will dramatically increase your sense of personal power and your self-confidence, and your trading and personal life will improve as a result.

If you are reading this and pointing a finger at someone else who is a complainer, rather than discussing with him that he is a complaine hand him this chapter.

## CONCLUSION

Complaining is a losing strategy for traders, resulting in a decline in your sense of personal power and self-confidence, and ultimately affects your bottom line. But, complaining as a way of life can be transformed into a new way of looking at yourself as a committed problem solver. This empowering new strategy has the potential to lift you out of a dead-end way of conducting your professional and personal affairs. Through the passage of time and a century of research into the human condition, it appears that this is what Disraeli meant when he advised, "Don't complain, don't explain."

PART III

# Taking Right Action

*Making consecutive good choices will snowball you into a momentum of more good choices.*

CHAPTER 16

# The Momentum of Choices

$E = MC^2$ *(Energy = Momentum × Choices*$^2$*)*

Don't be afraid. This chapter is not about physics. It is, however, a chapter about how to create success in life.

If you want to be wildly successful in life, one of the most important keys to achieving success is to create momentum—that powerful force of movement forward—that literally pulls and pushes you to success, despite obstacles in the way and despite the drag of negative forces. Momentum is not magic but it can appear to be magical when it takes hold of a person's path to success. However, there is nothing magical about the creation of momentum. Every inch of success that results from momentum can be measured by the choices that you make along the way.

## ADDING UP THE CHOICES

During our day, we are confronted with choices. For example:

- Should we get up now and do that early morning run or get 20 more minutes of sleep?
- Should we grab that donut for breakfast or sit down for a healthy meal?

- Should we pay that old bill or take the money and go out for an expensive dinner with friends?
- Should we watch our favorite television show or spend the time helping our son with his math homework?

The list goes on and on and on. We are making choices when we are not aware of making them, and we are making choices when we choose to do nothing.

You can think of your life as a series of savings accounts. Each time you make a choice, you are putting capital in one of your accounts. One account is for your future, and one is for your health, and one is for your family, and one is for your career, and one is for your education. On the other hand, you can also have accounts that have increasing balances for your ill-health, or an account for your poverty, or one for your increasing waistline, or one for your deteriorating property value, or one for your future loneliness, or one for your future unemployment, or one for your addictions.

Over time, these accounts add up. Each deposit you make in an account creates momentum in that direction. The bigger the account, the more weight it has to pull you in a particular direction. As your education account increases, it has more and more force to pull you in the direction of success in life, because educated people have more knowledge, which gives you more power, authority, and influence. The more choices you make each day, however, to feed your addictions, the more power they have to move you in a completely different direction. The momentum of these choices will move your life toward self-destruction, loss, poverty, social isolation, and illness.

In an interview with a television reporter, the actor Vin Diesel talked about his road to success. When he was in his early twenties living in New York City, Vin and his friends were all trying to become actors. At night, after their daytime jobs, they would all go out and party. Vin, however, stayed home and studied and prepared to become an actor. He made the choice each night to commit to his future. His friends, in an attempt to influence his decision to stay home, ridiculed and teased him. However, Vin continued to make the choice each night to put energy into his education and career accounts. It took time for these accounts to build up momentum. But, eventually, they were large enough to create enough momentum to get his career rolling.

You can argue that Vin is not your favorite actor, that he is not a great talent, or that he does not get the most challenging roles. The fact is that Vin kept making the choices that created enough momentum to move him in the direction he dreamed of going. On the other hand, none of his old friends ever made it as actors. Their choices did create momentum, but not in the right direction.

## THE CHOICE TO TURN LEMONS INTO LEMONADE

Any choice we make can turn out to be life altering. We can choose to take an airplane flight that terrorists board and steer into the World Trade Towers. Or we can choose to sit in the front row of a history class in college right next to a student whom we eventually marry. Or we can choose to get our flu shot on the day just before the supplies run out and we survive a flu pandemic while others do not. Those are serendipitous choices.

The most important choice with which we are all confronted is what to do with the hand we are dealt. No one gets to choose whether to have blue or brown eyes, whether to have long shapely legs or short stubby ones, or to have an IQ of 150 or an IQ of 110. We do not get to choose our families or the country or neighborhood into which we are born. We do not get to choose whether we will be born with beautiful bone structure in our faces or whether we will develop chinless faces with eyes that are too close and teeth that come in at all angles. Life is not fair and we get what we get.

Based on the hand you are dealt in life, here are some of the choices you can make:

- If you are blessed with good fortune (i.e., good health, good looks, high intelligence, loving parents, material comfort, education, a stable and free society) you can make any one of these negative choices of:
  - Taking for granted your good fortune and squandering it
  - Abusing your body and your mind with addictive substances
  - Complaining that your life is not perfect enough and that you don't have everything
  - Feeling a sense of entitlement and expecting to be given everything, and feeling the right to take whatever you want
  - Feeling guilt for your good fortune and sabotaging it in order to lessen your feelings of guilt

  Or you can make some of these positive choices of:

  - Feeling gratitude for your good fortune, treasuring it, and caring for it
  - Sharing your good fortune with others less fortunate
  - Using your good fortune to create more good fortune
- If, however, you are dealt a hand with misfortune, you can make the negative choices of:
  - Feeling sorry for yourself for your poor fortune
  - Feeling angry and making others pay for what you do not have

- Hurting yourself further by failing to care for yourself and by sabotaging yourself

Or you can make some of the positive choices when you are dealt a tough hand to play:

- Feeling gratitude for the blessings you do have
- Identifying your strengths and developing them further in order to offset your weaknesses
- Finding creative ways to overcome or reverse your lack or limitations
- Taking care of yourself in order to build a stronger foundation

I have worked with a number of individuals who were born with severe handicaps, some of which would be the perfect reason for never attempting to do anything in life but wait to die. Because I am a success coach, these particular individuals came for coaching because they had a commitment to reaching their full human potential, regardless of their physical limitations. They had simply made the decision to make lemonade out of lemons.

Last year, a seminar promoter who was putting together a major symposium in England invited me to be one of the principle speakers. I accepted the invitation and promptly made plans to attend. Unfortunately, the promoter was forced to reschedule the program, but assured me that the newly scheduled symposium would be a great success. Thus, after recouping a loss on my first flight reservation, I bought a second ticket and made new hotel reservations.

A week and a half before I was to leave for the symposium, I received word that it was cancelled. My flight was not refundable and I was committed to going. I had been dealt a lemon and I chose to turn it into lemonade. That choice provided me with the energy and determination I needed to make phone calls and write emails to people in London who might be interested in hearing me speak. Before I knew it, I had more than enough lemonade than I needed to cover my expenses and to compensate me for the loss of revenue I had expected from the trip. In fact, it turned out that the cancellation of the original speaking engagement was a good thing, resulting in a far better outcome for me than I would have had without the cancellation.

There are no guarantees that you will always be able to turn your lemons into lemonade. If you fail, you will still be left with lemons. If you succeed, you will never be sorry you took the risk. However, whether you succeed or fail, the decision to take positive action will create momentum in the right direction. The decision to wallow in your losses can only create momentum in a negative direction.

## INCREASING THE MOMENTUM OF YOUR CHOICES

So, now that you can see the benefits of making the right choices, how do you get started? Follow these six steps.

1. The first step to increasing the momentum of your choices is to be aware that you are making choices. This step is not as easy as it sounds. We make most of our choices unconsciously and/or automatically. As you take various steps during the day, just be aware that each one reflects a choice, and just acknowledge to yourself that you have just made a choice and what it was.
2. Now that you are aware of the act of making choices throughout the day, start asking yourself what choices you would really like to make in various parts of your life. For example, what choices would you like to be making in your career, in your home life, in your marriage, in your public life, in your health and well being, in your financial life, and so on?
3. If you are unable to see what choices are available to you, then sit down and write out a plan for your life. What are your goals? What kind of life do you want to have? One of the fastest ways to find out what you really want from your life is to write out your own eulogy. Pretend that you have reached the end of your life. What do you *want* to say about your life and how you lived it. This is not the time to censor your thoughts, but to let them take flight.
4. Now list the choices you will have to make to create that life you would like to live. Take a look at them. You might just want to start with a few choices that are easy to make, and then, once you have incorporated those easy choices into your daily life, you can take on bigger challenges.
5. Remember: Rome was not built in a day. It was built in tens of thousands of days. All great achievements are the result of things that were done each day—often very small things that were done each and every day. So, make certain that you make those small positive choices each time, every day.
6. Now that you have decided which choices you want to make, reward yourself each time you make a good choice. Rewarding yourself when you make positive choices will reinforce your decision to make those choices. That reinforcement will help you to make those choices automatically. Automatic positive choices are the best ones to make. They build the kind of momentum that is unstoppable.

## CONCLUSION

How can you tell if your choices are creating momentum? That's easy. Just look at the results. You are building momentum when opportunities begin to look for you and not the other way around. You are on a momentum roll when you feel good about yourself, when you have energy, when you feel positive and motivated, and when you can see success within reach because you are achieving small goals along the way. Momentum builds over time, so do not expect to be steamrolling toward your success immediately. Just remember that each time you make a choice that supports your goals, you are adding to your momentum. The more deposits of positive choices you make into your goal accounts, the faster you will see progress toward your goals.

---

*One of the best ways to learn a lesson is to take action.*

---

CHAPTER 17

# Action Is the Bottom Line

After many years of working with some of the finest traders in the world, I have arrived at the conclusion that it is not what traders say but what they do that makes the difference between failure and success. If taking the right action is the key to making money for a trader, then the question becomes: What leads a trader to take that action?

## PERCEPTION AS REALITY

The phone rings. On the other end of the line is a trader who tells me with pride in his voice that he is trading with a modest amount of capital. He also tells me that his wife and family are supportive of his efforts and that he will do whatever is necessary to be successful. Later that day, I hear from another trader who comes into trading with five times the capital of the first trader. However, he does not see himself as having adequate resources to make the personal investment that is needed to become a top trader. He feels that his family is unsupportive and he debates about the time and money that will be required to continue his education as a trader. The first trader is well on his way to success, while the second has placed roadblocks directly in his own path. The first trader can take positive action, while the second trader hesitates.

What makes the difference between these traders? The difference is not financial resources, but the perception of what those resources are. How you see yourself and others will largely determine the actions that follow. It is those actions that will create the rewards that you reap. The traders who know how to measure what is needed and will pay the required price are the traders who will ultimately become successful. If they perceive their needs and see the value in meeting those needs, then they are motivated to act. But first, they must have a clear vision of all that they have and all that they could be.

## WHAT SCHMIDT COULDN'T SEE

I saw the movie *All About Schmidt.* It is an excellent story filled with many good lessons for traders. Schmidt was an insurance agent facing retirement who must come to grips with lifelong patterns of selfish and negative thoughts and actions. Just before his wife dies, Schmidt observes how all of his wife's habits are growing especially annoying to him. He buries her in a cheap casket, which is an act that is consistent with his treatment of her in their marriage. Schmidt's final connection with his wife is in stark contrast to the widowed psychiatrist in the film, *Good Will Hunting*, where Robin Williams' character reveals that his wife's idiosyncrasies made him love her even more.

The enduring lesson to be learned from *All About Schmidt* is the tragedy of not appreciating what we have until we lose it. After his wife died, Schmidt began to miss her and to appreciate all that he had lost. Throughout his life, he had been a taker and not a giver. But, the day after his wife died, he watched a televised appeal from a charity to give $22 a month to support a poor child from another country. Then, he received a request from the same charity in the mail. For reasons he could not understand, Schmidt felt compelled to take on this small obligation. He received the news that he had adopted a six year old to whom he could write if he chose to do so. The $22-per-month relationship that developed between Schmidt and this child eventually brought him the greatest rewards of his life. The irony is that had he invested his love and attention in his wife and daughter while he had the opportunity, he wouldn't have been left alone, needing the love of a six-year-old child from a foreign country.

## REFLECTIONS—YOURS AND OTHERS

Because our perception of who we are and what we possess shapes our actions, it is especially helpful to understand our perceptions before we can begin to change them. One way to understand who we really are versus our self-perception is by seeing our reflection in the perceptions that others have of us.

For example, some traders may see themselves as lacking success and happiness because they have been experiencing a difficult period in their trading. This may be in contrast to the perception of others who observe their wonderful home lives, loving families, and comfortable lives. This would lead them to conclude that these same traders are highly successful, happy, and fortunate people. Which perception is the more accurate one? If we take the picture of our lives and look at it from an even greater distance of, say, the sub-Saharan African continent, we suddenly see our lives from a completely different perspective. Now, we can see the big picture and our lives look completely different.

One way to gain perspective on your life is to take the following exercise:

Step 1. Ask yourself what you think of your life: Are you happy? Successful? Does your life have meaning to you? What are your personal strengths and weaknesses and what are the strengths and weaknesses of your situation in life? What are your resources and what do you lack? What do you want and need to make you happier, more successful, more secure?

Step 2. Now, how would your friends, family, and associates describe you and your situation in life?

Step 3. How do you want to be seen?

Step 4. How would you and your life be viewed from the wealthiest European capitals? From the plains of Sudan? From the factories of Thailand? From the teeming streets of Rio de Janeiro?

When you are feeling badly about yourself, you have to look at reality and not compare yourself to people who have everything—or whom you perceive to have everything. Of course, this exercise views your life from the outside and describes what you have and not what is inside.

## TURNING ON A DIME

Traders live with the understanding that life turns on a dime. One day you are on top of the world. Then, faster than you can say "dot-com," you can lose it all. If you doubt the truth of this statement, you simply have to reflect on the fortunes or misfortunes of Martha Stewart and Ted Turner. One day, Martha Stewart was the maven homemaker/empire builder. She was the wealthiest woman in the United States. The next day, she found herself embroiled in an insider-trading scandal that resulted in the loss of her fortune, control of her company, plus her freedom when she faced a prison sentence. She has since come back to regain most of her wealth.

Ted Turner, one of the wealthiest men in the communications industry and noted philanthropist, suddenly lost 90 percent of his billions and became merely a pauper multi-millionaire. He is now back to his billion dollar status as well. These two stories only deal with the loss of fortune and fame. Consider the extraordinarily handsome and athletic actor Christopher Reeve, the star of the Superman movies. One day, he was astride a powerful horse playing polo with the rich and leisured. Moments later, he is was paralyzed, unable to speak, move a finger, and later died after a long battle resulting from that accident.

## YOUR PERSONAL RESOURCES

When your life has turned on a dime, the only way to climb out of the deep pit into which you have fallen is to be able to take action. The action that you take must be positive action that is taken in a timely way and not action that comes too late to reverse permanent damage. But, how do you get mobilized in time? If an individual has lost most of his material resources, many traders conclude that they are helpless. This is not the case. Many traders who have experienced devastating losses have rebounded to exceed their previous successes. How? They drew from within and took action.

Your personal resources are the tools that you have to rely upon in order to pull yourself out of the pit of misfortune. These resources are your perception of yourself and the relationships that you have formed as a foundation for your life. In the case of Christopher Reeve, who lost virtually everything, during his rehabilitation, he was able to draw upon his enormous emotional strengths and his equally enormous wealth of love, friendship and goodwill that he had established in his life. Based on that foundation of support, he was able to improve his situation. He could not give in to despair because he had too many others pulling for him when his own spirit flagged. Unfortunately, even with all of this, his body failed him.

Here is a brief exercise that will help you to assess your own inner resources:

- How do you see yourself in all the roles you play as a human being, husband, father, and trader?
- If others were to comment on your life and how you live it, what would they say?
- How do you see your childhood, teen years, and adult life?

## LISTING YOUR ASSETS

When you mobilize to take action, you need to use all of your assets. In addition to your relationships, you have other assets that make up your personal resources. These assets include your:

- Good health—good health is one of your greatest assets. Once you have lost it, the cost of replacing it can require the expenditure of all of your other assets.
- Status in your family and community—respect and a sense that you are an important and influential individual is the equivalent of capital in many situations, especially those that involve negotiation.
- Talents and abilities—these gifts allow you to accomplish things that individuals without them can only dream of doing. They are also resources that you can use to rebuild your life.
- Education and training—the effort you have put into developing your mind is money in the bank. None of the time and hard work that you have put into your education is wasted if you understand what you have learned and how to apply it.
- Attitude—if you are living as if it were so, you are able to mobilize all of your other assets to achieve your goals and take the right action.

When you begin to list your assets, your perception of your situation can change instantly. Suddenly, you will feel empowered. The sense of empowerment that comes from acknowledging your resources will propel you from a state of hopelessness and inertia to a state of action so smoothly and effortlessly that you will not be aware of the transition until after it has taken place.

## CONCLUSION

What does changing your perception have to do with making money? Ultimately, it is your perception, the perception of your glass being half full and not half empty that determines the action you decide to take. And action is the bottom line: the decision to take the risk—to take the action—to be successful. Action is what brings about change, what pulls you out of a slump, what corrects the losses, and what makes the money.

---

*The quality of decisions that you make for your trading and your life are based on your psychological foundation. If the foundation has cracks, so will your decisions.*

---

CHAPTER 18

# Traders and Decisions

What are some of the factors that affect your ability as a trader to make good decisions? Are there underlying issues that are preventing you from making the level of decisions that will help you to realize your dreams?

## I REALLY DON'T WANT TO SUCCEED

No one ever says that they don't want to succeed! And yet, that is one of the principle motivations for making poor decisions. It is difficult for anyone to know or admit on a conscious level that he is sabotaging his espoused goals. Most of the time, we simply cannot see what is actually happening. We are so busy telling ourselves and others that we are ambitious, motivated, and hungering for success. But underneath all of the bravado can be a fearful or guilty or self-loathing child who does not believe that he can or should attain his goals.

A childhood filled with instability, poverty and want, anger and violence, or constant criticism can create in the unconscious mind of an adult trader a comfort zone that does not include images of a successful life or the attainment of his dreams.

Sometimes, however, the underlying cause of a trader's failure to create a self-image of success can arise from a single traumatic incident in his developing years. Often, a trader has put the memory of that incident so far out of his consciousness that he does not even recall it. The loss of a competition, the breakup of a first romance, the public criticism by a teacher or authority figure—these are all potential deal breakers for anyone who is particularly vulnerable emotionally at that moment.

For a trader, one of those experiences that can undermine your image of yourself as a decision maker is a devastating loss from a trading mistake. Failure to pull the trigger on your potential trades can be the result. The perpetual second guessing that results from a bad decision can turn a once-confident decision maker into a fearful one who sees himself as a failure.

## INADEQUATE EARLY MODELS

We are rarely conscious of the models we set firmly in our unconscious of the lives we should be living, since we tend to do this when we are very young. Traders who grow up in unstable circumstances may have modeled on parents or peers who continue to make poor choices in life.

One of the ways to discover who your models may actually be is to ask yourself whose life yours most closely resembles. The answer may come as a great surprise, either a pleasant or shocking one! If you see your life unfolding like that of a person in your life who is living a happy and successful life, then you are on the right track. But, if you can see that you are making the same choices as someone whose life is not a happy and successful one, then you need to be working on finding and developing a different model for your life.

## LACK OF EXPERIENCE

Traders who grew up in very protective homes are sometimes unprepared to make good decisions because they were never given the opportunity to do so when they were growing up. Parents who want to protect their children from pain and loss will make all the important decisions for them. The problem with this kind of protection is that a child never learns how to make a decision and how to judge the potential consequences of his decisions and then to experience them. Feedback from both good and bad decisions early on is a great education for a future successful trader.

If your parents were willing to let you make decisions while giving you some guidance in the process, then you will find that, although you will not always make the perfect decision, you are able to do so with confidence. And afterward, if the decision turns out to have negative consequences, you will know how to deal with them without turning your mistakes into a reason for self-sabotage in the future.

However, if you are inexperienced in making decisions, you may feel overwhelmed, frightened, or simply unprepared to do so. Like learning how to swim, drive, write, or draw, there is only one solution to learning how to make good decisions: You need to find yourself a good teacher or coach and then practice, practice, practice. You will need to be willing to make mistakes and learn from them.

## DECISION-MAKING OVERLOAD

I once met a retired air-traffic controller who wanted to trade. He described the incredible stress he had been under and the thousands of potentially life and death decisions he made over the course of a single day. Because he had worked far beyond the amount of time he was supposed to work in his previous profession, his entire nervous system was destroyed. Overwhelmed with anxiety, his hands shook uncontrollably and he was no longer able to work in any capacity. His life was a living example of the effects of making too many decisions. Much later, I read an article about the limits of the human mind to make decisions in any set period of time and the effect an overload can have on the nervous system.

Traders who attempt to work long hours, pushing themselves past their decision-making tolerance, run the risk of overloading their nervous systems. Like our air-traffic controller, a trader can be aware that each decision has the potential for great loss or success. The result can then be an inability to make any decisions. On the other hand, traders who are careful not to push themselves to their limits are able to make the best decisions because they come to the process refreshed, full of energy, and with the ability to focus.

## CONCLUSION

These are some of the factors that affect your ability to make good decisions. If you recognize yourself in any of them, you have work to do. If you find that you are not able to do this work alone, find yourself a qualified counselor or coach to help you overcome the underlying issues that are preventing you from making the level of decisions that will help you to realize your dreams.

---

*When you make good choices, the new and improved you will emerge.*

---

CHAPTER 19

# The Big Reveal

Several years ago I was walking down the street in Geneva, Switzerland, looking in the jewelry shops. My focus was on what I could not afford. There was a part of me thinking about those who could purchase whatever they wanted. I decided to change my focus by asking myself, "What would I buy, if I had the money to purchase anything I wanted?" The shift was quite dramatic when I allowed myself to afford. What I found was that I was just as discriminating, but enjoyed the process more. I purchased a bracelet that I could and would purchase at any level of my net worth and did not feel that I was settling.

What if you gave up the idea that you did not presently have the resources to be the kind of trader that you wanted to be? What action would you start to take? Or, what is really behind your not taking action?

## YOU REALLY DO NOT WANT TO DO THE WORK

Not having money is a good reason for you not to start taking any action on accumulating the knowledge and doing the necessary planning to become an accomplished trader. Let's face it: One of the only reasons that you want to trade is that it looks like an easy way to earn a huge amount of money with very little effort. At least that is what is beneath the surface of your thinking. What you really want is someone to give you the trades to take because studying the fundamental and technical side of trading is quite boring and/or tedious to you, and besides you do not understand it.

You are the kind of person that would be attracted to a software program where you do not have to know anything except to push a button when certain colored lines cross. Just as an aside, those who have tested out these types of programs have found that a coin toss works just as well. You perhaps have thought, "If only someone would hire me and train me. After all, is it not discrimination for institutions to only consider hiring those who have college degrees from Ivy League schools for those kind of positions?"

One such trader was John who worked as a router for a trucking company for 20 years. His wife handled the family accounting, which in her case meant that the family did not have any savings. When the company John worked for started downsizing, the family went into a panic. John considered what else he could do to support his family. His thoughts were directed to cousin Ray who earned a comfortable living as an equity trader. Ray gave John some books and magazines.

John heard about an Expo for trading that was going to be in Southern California. He and his wife trucked to the event. John's wife was more intrigued by all the free promos that were being given out until she started listening to a presenter who was speaking about software that would make them millions with very little effort. John, not being able to understand any of the speakers, was grateful to his wife when she pointed out this simple way to make money in the markets. They put down their credit card to purchase the software for $5,000.

Several months later cousin Ray decided to expand his business and asked John if he would like to be considered as a trader trainee. At first John was as ecstatic as if he were already hired and earning money. Then Ray said "Bring in the books I gave you, so we can discuss them." John knew that even if he delayed the meeting he could not understand the books enough to even ask questions. It is interesting how he knew this without even opening up a book.

Fortunately, John had not lost his job yet, because he would need it to pay off both the debt of the software and the additional $3,000 that he had lost so far using that software. The fact is that John did not have the confidence and passion to create the drive necessary to become a trader, even when a good opportunity was handed to him.

## YOU DO NOT WANT TO SIT IN FRONT OF A COMPUTER SCREEN ALL DAY

Sitting at a desk and watching a computer screen for you is like watching wet paint dry. Being a part-time observer of the markets is fun, like playing a computer game. But you have come to realize that full-time trading is not necessarily a full-time eight hour day; it is making full-time money. Even though you might have heard this before, your work ethic will not allow you to think or act that way.

Mark, a successful lawyer, was happy to hear me say on a Webinar that he could make full-time money in a few hours a day from trading. He actually held off his retirement because he was afraid that he would be compulsive about sitting in front of the screen. When I gave Mark permission on my Webinar to work two hours a day, not long after he handed in his resignation. Now he is enjoying trading and retirement as well. Mark needed to choose the kind of trading and hours that would work for him. Actually, it was not my giving Mark permission that lit a fire under him; it was his willingness to give himself that permission.

## YOU DO NOT WANT THE RESPONSIBILITY

Being responsible with a job that pays you a reliable salary is not the same as being responsible and not knowing if you will earn any profits from trading. With most people losing in the markets, it is no wonder that they come to the conclusion that trading is gambling. Any responsible person would not want to be a gambler with his hard-earned money.

Jack did all the right things to become a trader, but he could not get his family's beliefs out of his head that trading was gambling. He attended one of my seminars where he met several professional traders. This was enough to change his belief. Jack took a leave of absence from his job and never looked back. He started looking at the larger picture beyond receiving a weekly paycheck. Jack learned that professional trading could be a responsible career if you make the right choices and align yourself with the right kind of thinking.

## YOU ARE AFRAID OF BEING WRONG AND/OR AFRAID TO FAIL

Making choices to become a trader, to settle on a particular strategy, to risk hard-earned money is not comfortable for many because they could be wrong about their choices. Being wrong and learning how to self-correct is not part of how many people operate. It is just too uncomfortable. Someday, which does not exist as a day of the week, becomes their mantra.

I met Allen six years ago at a trading conference. Since then, he has been returning to my booth as a loyal follower ever since. He was a "Someday" kind of "wanna-be trader" for a few years. Then he was a "getting close to kind of trader," then an "almost there kind of trader" for the next few years. I will most likely see Allen again in a few months and wonder what he will say then.

Allen has consumed a library of trading books, CDs, and courses over the years that would rank with the best of trading libraries. With this kind of knowledge you would think that he would be a well-established professional trader. The fact is that he is even afraid of simulated trading, because Allen's problem is that he does not want to be wrong. He is afraid of working with me because he might be the one person that does not get results from my coaching. So Allen will most likely remain a "Someday" trader.

## YOU REALLY DO NOT WANT TO OR ARE AFRAID OF LEAVING YOUR PROFESSION

You loved your profession, but it has changed over the years to something you now do not enjoy. Trading is an escape from what you do not want, but it is not what you really want. You want your profession to be the way it was.

This is true for so many doctors as well as lawyers, engineers, senators, presidents, and accountants. The promise of an exciting career when you were in college did not turn out to be what you have experienced in the real world. Perhaps it could have been good in the beginning, but because of changing times it just is not the same. Trading becomes the new passion for you, but you are afraid that it, too, might just turn out to be another disappointment.

Anna wanted to be a doctor from when she was a child. She was compelled by the thought that she could help people in their darkest hours and that is the way she wanted to live her life. Coming from a blue-collar environment where her family lived from paycheck to paycheck, the promise of the affluent lifestyle of a doctor was also part of the dream.

Anna was not the kind of person to enjoy the back office side of running a business. She settled on working with a partnership of family doctors. Anna was to spend no more than 15 minutes with each patient and not discuss more than two issues. Her computer was her constant companion, needing it to remember patients and document every word that they said. This was not the family doctor she pictured herself to be watching *Dr. Quinn, Medicine Woman* on television as she grew up. And with not only that stifling her dreams, because Anna's student loans were ever present, her lifestyle was not what she had hoped for.

A patient introduced Anna to trading. Anna felt that at least in trading there was the hope to accomplish one of her dreams. In her spare time Anna worked on becoming a trader but realized that she could not successfully do both.

It has been several years since Anna's struggle. I am happy to report that she married a doctor and works part time in his office. She manages the family's finances as a trader and lives an enviable lifestyle. It is important to note that Anna did what was necessary to become a trader even though it was not apparent to her at the time how she could make it work. It reminds me of the movie *Field of Dreams*, when it was said, "Build it and they will come." She made trading happen and then opportunity presented itself.

## BECOMING A TRADER WILL DEVASTATE YOUR FAMILY

There are many parents who sacrifice for their children, but sometimes this comes with a price. They expect and encourage their children to either live the life that they wanted for themselves, or live a life that they want them to live for other various reasons. When their offspring display the kind of independence that the parents have had in their lives, all hell can break loose.

Sammy was given everything he wanted. He was the golden child that could do no wrong. Sammy's brother became an athlete with no form of income of his own. His sister married after graduating with an art degree with a goal of having a life of leisure. Sammy knew what was expected of him after college and dutifully ran his father's business for five years. He married the kind of woman that his family expected him to marry and they had the two expected children.

Sammy's friend introduced him to trading and it was love at first sight. He became obsessed and that obsession turned to earning good money, but it was at the cost of the business beginning to fail. Sammy started to sabotage his efforts in trading when his father had a heart attack. He blamed himself and everyone blamed him as well. This is when I entered the picture. I worked with Sammy on balancing his life to include both the business and his trading. Sammy's brother and sister entered the business on a part-time basis and finally found that they came from the same cloth as their father, enjoying working fulltime. Sammy was then able to give more time to his trading and not feel guilty. While this is a happy ending, most of these situations are not.

Evaluate yourself by answering these questions:

- What is behind the veil? It is important that you know why you want to become a trader and what is sabotaging each new level of success.
- What would happen if you had the money and time to be a trader right now? By having an action plan of all the things you need, you will be on your way. If you wait to plan and study, then even if you have the money and time you will not be ready when the time comes.
- What are the excuses that you give others and yourself for why you are not trading or not trading to your ability? By being honest with yourself, you might find out that you really do not want to be a trader. Or, you might find that the self-sabotage issues you face can be overcome with the right help.

## CONCLUSION

Trading is not for everyone. You must love all stages of the process to have the passion, drive, commitment, and discipline necessary to succeed. Opportunity is available for those who are committed to making things happen.

*Rules are for those who want to progress. Following those rules are for those who have what it takes to succeed.*

CHAPTER 20

# The Rules of the Game

A young trader named David is about to lose his job and does not see the end coming. Losing his job will be a great personal, professional, and financial blow. Because of his loss, he will probably lose his apartment and his credit score will fall. It will take him a long time to get back on his feet. I happen to be friends with the top management of the company where he works and I am privy to his impending fate, but I am unable to warn him.

The two questions that have been nagging at me for days are:

1. How did this happen?
2. And why is he unaware of it?

Actually, I know the answer to both of these questions. The answer is that despite all of his hard work and good intentions, David has failed to play by the rules of the game he is playing.

## THE PLAYERS AND THE CLUELESS

Every human endeavor operates on the basis of a set of unwritten rules. In the modern world, we often resist the notion that we must adhere to a set of rules that we did not establish. Each of us has the illusion of being in control of our lives, but those who are streetwise are well aware of the nature of the games, what is at stake, and what the rules are. These savvy men and women are the players. The rest of the participants in the games of life are the clueless ones. These are the individuals who fail to understand that they are playing a game, what the rules are, and the consequences of not playing by those rules.

No game I know of is as cruel to the clueless as the school playground. From personal observation, it appears that some of us are hardwired to catch on early (the players) and others are hardwired to never catch on (the clueless). Players do not chafe against the rules. They learn them, master them, and win most of the games they play.

In the prestigious company where David works, the unwritten rule is that it does not matter how much money you are making for the clients. What matters is how well you communicate with them. David is a very good trader who has consistently made a respectable return for his company's investors. Unfortunately, he is a particularly poor communicator.

To make matters worse, he does not see the point of being a good communicator. Despite all of the advice he has received about returning calls to the company's clients to provide them with updates and feedback, David sees it as a waste of his time—time that is better spent doing his research and making better trades. One could easily assume that the bottom line is what the investors care about most, but in this particular game, one would be wrong.

Although each game has its own rules, there are some general rules that should always be kept in mind. Sadly, David has flaunted nearly all of these general rules, to say nothing of the specific ones. Here are 10 of the rules:

1. Every human endeavor is played out like a game and each has its own rules that are specific to it.
2. Do not assume that you know what the rules are—especially if you are applying logic or past experience to a new game. Learn the rules of the game you are playing.
3. If you want to find out what the rules are, look for the most successful player and study him. He will be a master player.
4. Develop relationships with the successful players. Ask them for advice and seek their protection until you become a skillful player.
5. Step into the game slowly and only after much preparation and practice. Do not leap into the game unprepared.
6. Bring enough chips to the game so that you are not forced to leave the table before you have learned how to play.
7. Make a clear list of the rules in your head and/or on paper so you know what they are. Then, set them to memory.

8. Commit to following these rules, as you understand them. Acknowledge the cost of not following them.
9. If you decide that you do not like the game and do not want to play by its rules, be very clear that you must leave the game.
10. Never whine because you were forced to leave the game for failing to play by its rules.

There is no shame in leaving a game when you do not like or agree with the rules. Find a game where you can excel and the rules are consistent with your values. On the other hand, no points are ever awarded for being clueless or for staying that way. David is a nice young man who flaunted the most sacred rule of his organization and he will soon be paying the price. My hope is that someday he will seek me out as his coach and I will be able to teach him how to play any game he chooses and emerge as a winner.

If trading is a game that has its own rules, and if washing out of trading is the price you pay for failing to play by those rules, exactly what are those rules?

I have listed below five of the most important general rules of trading as a profession. These rules are not the technical rules that can be mastered through reading, taking a few courses, and practice in paper trading. Nor are they the trading rules that you will develop for entering and exiting trades. These are the rules of the game that allow you to enter the game and stay in it long enough to become a successful professional. Here are the rules:

1. In trading, the winner takes all because trading is a zero-sum game. There are no second or third place prizes handed out in trading. There is nothing warm and fuzzy about the markets. For people who have played in arenas where an effort is made to support the loser and to humanize the game, this is a difficult and painful concept to wrap oneself around. There is much at stake in trading and losing can mean losing everything and being forced to leave the game. If this level of risk is unacceptable, you are getting a clear signal to find another game to play.
2. You cannot play to win without the admission price. This rule is another of the painful realities of trading. Attempting to trade without sufficient capital is the equivalent of fighting the U.S. military with slingshots or taking on the Mensa club with the patients from the Alzheimer's wing. Sufficient capital for entering trading falls in a range, with the very bottom being approximately $25,000 and no upper limit. This capital cannot be money that is needed to live on.
3. A new trader must have another source of income that can be counted upon to supply his family's needs for at least three years. You will hear

traders argue that these figures are too high, but they are the few who have survived. The others are already out of the game, having lost all their capital. If a trader is playing with too little capital, he will have no room to experience the losses and remain in the game. In addition, he will be playing scared, which is a little like dueling with both arms tied behind your back.

4. Preparation is required. The trader who has read everything, taken every course, attended every workshop, done endless research, developed his own trading system, back-tested it thoroughly, and paper-traded for an extensive period of time is a prepared trader. Match this prepared trader against a cowboy trader who is shooting from the hip without any target practice and you can apply rule number one. The professional can start counting his money before the first volley is fired.
5. Psychology is more important than smarts and/or formal education. I have worked with incredibly successful traders who did not make it through high school. What they had going for them, in each case, was the right psychology. And what is that? They were trading with confidence and focus with a sense of calm, with a love of the process, and without the baggage of fear, greed, and unresolved psychological issues that lead to self-sabotage.

This advanced state of psychological balance is rare. Some individuals are born with it, but most acquire this state through commitment, effort, the willingness to do the hard work and confront their fears, and the willingness to make the investment in money and time to deal with their issues. Here are six ways to deal with these issues:

1. Develop discipline. This rule is a subset of rule number four, but it is so important that it deserves its own category. Discipline is what motivates a trader to do the hard things that must be done rather than taking the easy way out, which, in trading, is usually the wrong way. Discipline allows a trader to say no to destructive behavior and yes to the scary things in trading like dealing with loss and money management.
2. Find a mentor or a trader to use as a model. The fastest way to learn all of the rules of trading and to become successful is to model a successful professional trader. Mentoring and modeling allows you to bypass all of the mistakes that novice traders make. It provides you with the authoritative guidance and support that breed confidence, which is key to successful trading.

3. Write a business plan. Traders with business plans are entrepreneurs and businessmen. Traders without business plans are just one step above gamblers and in some cases that one step can be eliminated. A business plan spells out all of the resources, trading methodology and/or rules, operational plans, budgets, money management, and feedback mechanisms that a trader uses to run his business. A well-written business plan signals to both the trader and to his family and associates that he is serious about being a professional. It is also the document that allows a trader to look for investors when the time comes to do so.
4. Take care and beware of your relationships. This is a complex rule because it advises a trader to make certain that his important relationships are in good health so they can support his professional life. Nothing can interrupt a successful trading career as quickly as a broken marriage. And this rule is also a warning to traders to let go of toxic, risky, and unsupportive relationships that can damage self-confidence and health and lead to risky behaviors.
5. Take care of your health. Far too many traders wash out of the game because they fail to apply this rule to their trading. Bad diets, lack of exercise and sleep, and too much stress all lead to the diseases and conditions that can end a career. I have counseled many floor traders disabled by stress-related illnesses as well as traders who can no longer work productively because of alcoholism, drug-taking, heart problems, and other disabling diseases.
6. Enjoy the process. There is no point in becoming a professional trader if you hate what you do and if each day drags on to the next. Find a way to enjoy the process or the process will find a way to end your career.

If you can master these 11 rules of the trading game, you are a ready to play to win.

## CONCLUSION

Those who make and follow their own rules and set rules for others who support them to follow, will always reap the rewards of this effort. Followed rules set a standard for becoming disciplined which is a necessary foundation for success.

---

*When you are in the "fight mode," you shut down being in the "zone mode."*

---

CHAPTER 21

# Getting Back at the Markets

Traders have two major reactions when the markets take back all of their earnings: They give up or they fight back. Neither works.

## SELF-DESTRUCTION

There are three main ways traders self-destruct.

### Walking Away

Sam was a professional trader for eight years. During that time, he successfully amassed a respectable fortune, at least by his standards. He moved his family into a beautiful home along the lakeshore, he bought two expensive cars, he sent his two children to private schools, and he took his family on exotic (if brief) vacations. If you asked Sam about his trading, he would wax poetic over his love for the profession and how he had learned to weather the vicissitudes of market reversals so that he could make a consistent profit over time. He had an impressive library of books on trading and he attended countless trading conventions and trading schools. His system was long in the development and well tested by him. At this point in his life, Sam was secure and did not have to trade to live his life-style for the rest of his life.

On the surface, Sam had done everything right and he was reaping the rewards. But, when Sam was caught in a major downturn that he was not expecting without having a physical stop, he was unable to move quickly enough and he panicked. The results were catastrophic for him. In the space of one day, Sam lost a significant amount of his trading capital and a significant amount of his pride. At this point he faced the conflict: Does he fold his hand or ante up?

## Fighting Back

Mel had never walked away from a defeat in his life. When he entered the trading profession, he had created a series of great successes in his wake. In each of these successes, Mel was forced to push his way through losses and defeats in order to reach his ultimate goals. When the chips were down, Mel came back fighting. He was a fighter who saw challenges in every difficulty, and opportunities in every challenge.

So, when Mel saw his positions going against him and was unable to get out of his trades in time, thereby sustaining a deep loss, he was in a fighting back mood. He was not going to back down. Instead, he immediately returned to his trading desk and put in another series of trades, ignoring the fact that his system was virtually screaming at him to stop. By the time Mel was done, he had traded his way to the bottom.

But, Mel was undeterred. Having lost nearly all of his trading capital, he went to his father-in-law and borrowed enough money to get back into the game. After all, he had never retreated from adversity, had always come out on top, and had a long track record of success to defend. His reputation was at stake. Having made a lot of money for his father-in-law in the past, Mel found it easy to persuade his wife's father to lend him the money.

So, Mel got back into the market. But suddenly, trading was different for him in undefinable ways, and before he knew what had happened, Mel had managed to lose his father-in-law's capital as well. Nevertheless, Mel was not a quitter. He was going to get in there and win. But how?

## Getting Back

Richard was neither a quitter nor a fighter. He was simply angry. It wasn't fair, it wasn't right, and he wasn't going to let those *blankety-blanks* get away with having taken his hard-earned savings in one fell swoop! Richard was going to get back at the markets. He had retribution on his mind when he went back to trading the next day. His anger propelled him into some seriously foolish trades, but he did not care. He was going to show those *blankety-blanks* out there a thing or two! Which is exactly what he did—instead of losing in an ordinary fashion, Richard managed to lose everything in a colossal fashion. Going out in a blaze of glory suited Richard much better than merely fighting back. But what did he gain?

## THE WHYS OF A LOSING STRATEGY

Why would a trader completely lose hope and give up? If he has lost all of his trading capital, it would seem like a reasonable way to cope: Start over in something new and find a way to rebuild your life. The problem is twofold:

1. When an individual walks away in defeat and does not find a way back into the game, he sets up a pattern of walking away from loss. Each time he faces a loss afterward, he will find himself walking away sooner and sooner. After a series of these experiences, he will be unwilling to take on any challenges for fear of failure.
2. Walking away in defeat erodes self-confidence. A high level of self-confidence is essential to successful trading. It is also the foundation of success in virtually every other walk of life as well.

Sam caved in and walked away in defeat because he had never had to deal with serious pain and loss. He did not have the experience of coming back from defeat, so he saw defeat as total and permanent. He would much rather cut his losses and avoid any further pain than attempt to get back into the game and suffer so much pain and fear ever again. But, there are three additional reasons for giving up, including:

1. **Lack of confidence.** A trader who lacks confidence is likely to give up when the going gets tough.
2. **Negative self-talk.** Most self-talk that is negative is really the echo of the critical and negative voices of significant others in a trader's life: parents, teachers, close friends and relatives, the voices that told a trader when he was young that he could not do it, that he would certainly fail, that life was hard, and so on.
3. **Pessimism.** Traders who unconsciously believe that they are not lucky, that bad things are the most likely to happen, that one small failure actually represents the totality of all experience, and that good things are the exception are pessimists. And pessimists are most likely to give up.

## FIGHTING BACK

Why would a trader fight back? He is likely to have learned in the past that fighting back is a successful strategy for overcoming adversity and obstacles in his way. He may have a running monologue in his mind that goes something like this: "I'm not a quitter. I never give up until I reach my goal." So, what is the problem with fighting back after a major loss?

- Fighting back without a carefully laid out plan of attack has never, in the history of warfare, guaranteed a victory. Far too many just causes have met with defeat because they were fought with a sense of righteousness and not from having the right plan. Brilliant strategists of the past who understood the nature of their opponent and the principles of warfare won their battles by having a good plan.
- There are some issues that need to be addressed after a major loss. By not taking the time to lick one's wounds, to figure out what went wrong, and to regroup one's psychology, the act of reactively fighting back is guaranteed to create more of the same.

  Fighting back is a healthy response to any attack. It indicates a high level of self-esteem, a feeling that you are worthy enough to defend, and a sense of optimism in the future. The only problem is that this reflexive strategy can backfire if it is put into practice in a volatile market in which all bets are off.

## GETTING BACK

Why would a trader want to get back at the markets, or at anything for that matter? Traders who respond with anger when things do not go their way usually have a well of anger that is filled to the top and erupts at the smallest provocation. In my experience, traders who respond with anger have deep-seated issues that have never been addressed. Their anger is not a healthy response; it is a habitual response that creates health problems. This anger is driven by certain feelings and worldviews that feed on each other. For example, a trader who is habitually angry:

- Feels, at a deep level, powerless and victimized; that is, he suffers from passivity and passive aggression.
- Believes that the world is out to get him and that it is an unfair world.
- Often comes from a dysfunctional home or social environment, in which the significant people in it were unable to solve their

own problems, create any success in their lives, or develop happy relationships.
- Has a need to even the score in life in order to feel better about himself.

Attempting to get back at the markets is a strategy perfectly designed to create self-sabotage and failure. By personifying the markets, a trader who wants to get back at them is caught in an emotional trap and is unable to see that the markets are not personalized. They do not feel and they do not care. The only one who will get hurt is the trader himself. Trading out of anger and a need for payback can only cloud a trader's judgment and focus, preventing him from following his rules and his money management: a sure prescription for further disaster.

## A BETTER STRATEGY

So, what is a trader to do when he has suffered a terrible loss? Here are some guidelines that I have developed over the years after coaching traders.

### Stop Trading

Stop trading, that is, until you have been able to work your way through the loss. One of the surest ways to heap disaster upon disaster is to push your way back into the game when you are suffering from a serious loss. Cessation of trading after a major loss is not the same thing as giving up. The cessation is temporary—a time for healing, regrouping, and planning. I frequently coach traders to stop trading temporarily after all kinds of unsettling experiences such as an accident, the sudden death of a loved one, a tremendous win in the markets, a separation or divorce.

Take time to analyze what happened. Did you go against your rules? If so, what were they, how did it happen, and what have you learned? How can you prevent this from happening again? Was your system at fault? If so, what can you do to update it? Do you need to redevelop it? Has the market changed to a degree that your trading methodology cannot make money? If so, what changes do you need to make in your trading to respond to changes in the markets?

Rework your business plan. Take time to go over your plan, update it, and improve it. This may involve reworking your trading system or methodology and your money management. Reworking your business plan will put new life into your trading business. It will also help you to refocus on what made you get into trading in the first place, how you can improve your performance, and what you can do to solve your current problems.

### Seek Out a Trader's Coach for Support and Guidance

If you can afford to pay for professional services, seeking out a trader's coach for support and guidance will be the most helpful to you. A good trader's coach can help you to:

- Deal with the psychological and self-sabotaging issues that are created by a painful loss
- Formulate a strategy to get you back to trading at peak performance
- Find the emotional support you need once you return to trading
- Deal with your family issues as you rebuild your business
- Deal with underlying psychological issues that may have contributed to your loss in the first place.

If you cannot afford to hire a trader's coach, find a support system to help you pull together your psychological issues so that you can get back to trading at peak performance. Find other traders like yourself—but only those who are optimistic and who have either returned to trading after a serious loss or who are planning their way back to their trading desk. Avoid pessimistic, depressed, and burnt-out associates with whom to spend your time.

### Build Your Health and Your Disciplines

While you are waiting to get back to trading, you will build your confidence if you also build up your energy reserves. Exercise, good sleep, a good diet, relaxation, and play can all have an amazing effect on your trading focus when you return to work.

Once you've done this, you can return to trading gradually. Do not plunge in. Create a plan and stick to it. Secondly, keep a log of your plans and your progress. Write in it daily. Finally, build small, measurable, and achievable goals and rewards into your daily schedule and plans. Nothing builds a sense of empowerment, self-confidence, and control like the steady achievement of small, measurable, and achievable goals.

## CONCLUSION

There is much you can do to respond appropriately and successfully to great loss, without resorting to self-sabotaging strategies and/or retreat. The ranks of the seasoned professional traders are filled with battle-scarred individuals who have faced loss and come back to trade another day.

*Transformation is instantaneous when a new belief is installed.*

CHAPTER 22

# What a Difference a Day Makes

Patrick was burned out. Over the past year, he had made a series of bad choices in his trading, his health, and his personal relationships. The results were predictable: serious losses in his trading, a lack of physical vitality with which to tackle his problems not to mention a festering depression that sapped his motivation, and a 10-year marriage headed straight for divorce.

A trader's success depends largely upon the small choices he makes every day and upon the results of his habits over time. When a trader changes his attitudes, beliefs, and decisions, a transformation takes place. Receiving a desperate call from Patrick, I sensed that he was ready to do whatever it took to make changes. I suggested that we start the process right away.

## TURNAROUNDS IN A SINGLE DAY

So, you are skeptical about the difference a single day can make in changing a bad situation. Well, Patrick certainly was until I told him some dramatic turnaround stories.

Over the years, I have helped countless traders to dramatically improve their trading by helping them to transform limiting beliefs, self-sabotaging behaviors and psychological issues, poor trading habits, and self-discipline problems. After a personal transformation during a private coaching session or a seminar, a fair number of traders have reported that their first day back trading produced a profound turnaround, with a new level of confidence, self-discipline, and ability to make exceptionally successful choices.

Nevertheless, here is one of my favorite stories of a turnaround for a trader. Mike was living in a studio apartment where he barely scraped out a living. The one thing he did have going for him was that he had a passion for trading and studied every book on trading that he could get his hands on. He had a system that produced extremely good results in simulation. The problem was he did not have any money to trade. He earned a good hourly sum in his part-time job but it was not enough to give him what he needed to trade.

When Mike completed my Trader's Evaluation, I suggested that he attend the Top Performance Seminar knowing that he did not have the money to pay the fee. He decided to borrow the money from his family in order to take the seminar. There were several people in the seminar who recognized his skill and decided that they would like to help him. They paid for his private consultation with me as well as giving him the seed money for trading capital and asked nothing in return. However, Mike felt obligated and decided to help the participants in the group with their trading. They formed a group and as a result of his good trading system and the psychology that they learned in the seminar, they all benefited by taking their own trading to a new level of profit.

## THE MOST POWERFUL ONE-DAY TURN-AROUND STEP

The act of making a decision is, in my experience, the single most powerful turn-around step that a trader can make. I am not referring to inconsequential decisions but the ones that can redirect your life, transform your performance, and significantly raise the level of your happiness and sense of personal fulfillment.

Making a decision sounds easy. "I've decided to climb Mt. Everest!" Declaring it aloud can be dramatic, but, if you are not committed to the decision, it is not actually a decision. It is merely a flight of fancy. A real decision requires commitment and commitment means taking action in the steady realization of the decision. So, just because you buy a book about mountain climbing, you may still not have made the decision.

A decision comes with a clear vision of it being brought into reality. That clear vision, in turn, causes you to feel a passion for making it happen. That passion, in turn, gives you the psychological and physical energy to do whatever it is you need to do to put your decision into action. The stories that I told Patrick all derived their success from the decisions that were made with conviction.

## WHY NOT MAKE A TURNAROUND DECISION?

If the mere act of making a decision to turn around a situation can start the ball rolling in the right direction that very same day, there should be a veritable stampede to be the first in line to make that life-altering decision. But, as far as I can see, there is no stampede. The problem is that the very people most in need of making a decision are the very ones least likely to do so. Why? If you find yourself unable or unwilling to make a decision to create a needed or wanted change in your life, perhaps you will see yourself in one or more of the following issues.

### "It's hopeless."

When things look especially bad, many traders are so overwhelmed with a sense of hopelessness that the very act of making a decision to turn the situation around is beyond their capacity to act. They lack the will because they no longer believe that they have the power to influence the outcome. Call it a failure of imagination, if you will. But, it also comes from a lack of perspective. When we are so close to a situation, we tend to be only aware of the problems, the failures, the obstacles, the pain, the loss, and the inevitable catastrophic end. If we can pull back and gain perspective, we may be able to see that the situation still has escape routes, solutions, or even opportunities embedded in it.

There is an old saying: When you get nervous, you get stupid! When people are filled with anxiety and fear, they are no longer able to access their creative intelligence. In the midst of a catastrophe, the most intelligent people can find themselves being led, like small children, by anyone who has been able to rise above the fear and lead them to safety.

Then, there is another element in the "it's hopeless" response that is essentially an excuse, a way to let you off the hook for taking action or responsibility. After all, if a situation is hopeless, then there is nothing you have to do. And, you will not have any responsibility in turning it around since there is no possible way to do so.

There is an even more disturbing underlying reason for using the "it's hopeless" response. Traders who unconsciously sabotage themselves are not really looking for a turnaround solution. Feelings of guilt and unworthiness are powerful motivators to create a situation that is hopeless and for which there is no solution.

### "I can't picture it!"

A decision that comes with sufficient commitment and passion to produce a turnaround must start with a picture of the final result. If you cannot create the mental picture, you will probably not be able to make the decision. Sometimes, the inability to create that mental image results from a trader not knowing what he actually wants. There may be underlying conflicts of which he is unaware. Perhaps part of him really wants to leave the profession of trading but is unable to admit it to himself. Or part of him wants to succeed but part of him is more comfortable with the images of loss. Or he may not be able to picture a good final outcome because he lacks faith in himself.

### "I don't have the time for this nonsense!"

In my experience, this response means that the trader feels threatened by the idea. This is a way of deflecting attention from what is really going on in the situation. Consider this: How much time does it really take to make a decision? A matter of seconds.

## TRANSFORMATIONS AND EPIPHANIES

Few of us have difficulty with the notion that life turns on a dime. We have all seen how quickly an act of nature can wipe away immense human structures built over a long period of time, or how quickly a fortune or reputation can disappear. Why is it so difficult to accept the fact that things can turn around that quickly in a single day? One of the first things I learned in my training in neuro-linguistic programming (NLP) was that transformations could be nearly instantaneous. When an old and deeply destructive mental association is replaced with a positive one, a trader is as instantly freed from the chains of his old self-destructive pattern as if he had been suddenly paroled from a life sentence. For example, when a trader has an unconscious association of pain and loss with change of any kind, he is unable to succeed in his profession out of fear of experiencing those feelings. But, if he can replace that negative association with one of adventure, hopefulness, and even joy, that same trader will suddenly be open to all manner of change. The same principle applies to epiphanies—those sudden realizations that alter one's basic understanding of one's life. I have seen traders come to sudden realizations that profoundly and instantaneously transformed their lives.

## CONCLUSION

What difference can a day make? Under the right circumstances, it can transform a losing situation into a winning one. Giving up is the option exercised by the depressed, the self-sabotager, the conflicted, and the frightened. The alternative to giving up is making a life-altering decision or undergoing a transformation or epiphany. What is holding you back? The answer is hidden inside you, but you may need help to find it.

PART IV

# Stretching and Expanding Yourself as a Trader

*Lessons learned are stepping stones to progress.*

CHAPTER 23

# Learning Something Every Day

One of the hallmarks of a great trader is his commitment to on-going learning and the continuous expansion of his understanding of the world around him. This commitment, when put into practice, becomes a daily discipline that keeps a trader's mind keen and able to maintain the focus essential to successful trading

The human brain is, technically, not a muscle, but it operates like a muscle in two important ways: First, it needs oxygen and nutrients, especially a continuous supply of blood sugar, to function, and second, it must be exercised continuously to avoid atrophy. The best way to keep your brain from going flabby is to continue to learn. But, before you put this principle into action, you need to ask yourself two questions: What should I learn and how should I learn it? The answers to these two questions can have profound consequences for your future.

## AN OPEN MIND VS. AN EMPTY ONE

Recently, I read a column from an expert in human development about the importance of learning every day. He went on to discuss the need for the individual to search out the truth for himself. Although this advice, on the surface, sounds logical and sound, it reminded me of the blind man whose experience of an elephant was feeling its trunk. His conclusion was that an elephant was long, thin, and round and exactly like a snake. If you are not a trained investigator of the truth, you can easily find yourself learning anything but the whole truth and then coming to the wrong conclusion. For a trader, that mistake could be ruinous.

Here are some guidelines I would like to offer you in your quest for an on-going search for learning and the truth. Please take them with the same measure of skepticism that I am suggesting you apply to all of your daily learning experiences.

### Apply a Healthy Dose of Skepticism to Everything You Learn

There are few things as pathetic as an individual spouting misinformation he recently read with trusting naiveté. Just remember that so many of the laws of nature that everyone knew to be true in the past have been proven wrong.

### Just 'Cause You Read It, Don't Make It So

These days, virtually anyone can get his opinions and his take on the truth into print. This dramatic expansion of the access to the printed media has become a double-edged sword. Without an editorial screening mechanism to check facts, sources, and a writer's own credentials, the most ill-informed individuals can have an audience. Furthermore, many newspapers and media sources that once exercised their editorial responsibilities have become hostage to the political and intellectual bullies who sit atop their organizations. For that reason, the best way to avoid the pitfalls of believing what you read is to read widely, getting your information from many disparate sources—very much like spreading the risk by diversification.

### Know Your Source

Understanding the story behind the story is important. For example, if you are reading some science journals that like to print articles that are the most "out in front," you need to be aware that some of them are written for the nonscientific community and do not apply the same stringent standards of peer review that other scientific journals do. The result is that, in recent times, they have retracted a higher proportion of these stories. Furthermore, when you read a story in the *New York Times* or the *Washington Post* from an "unnamed source" close to the story, it is important to remember that carefully developed information is planted with reporters by highly placed congressional aides and consultants who have a political agenda to support, regardless of which side of the fence they are sitting. This does not mean that the information is false, but it is usually just a piece of the story or is released for political purposes.

## Show Me the Money

Money often drives information. When a magazine or newspaper accepts large contributions to its support through advertising from specific industries, the content of their reporting on issues related to those industries is invariably compromised. Thirty years ago or more, you could read articles by a Harvard scientist named Dr. Frederick Stare about how beneficial eating lots of sugar was for your health. Years later, it was revealed that his nutrition institute was generously supported by the sugar industry. In the 1950s, the prestigious *Journal of the American Medical Association* remained on the fence about the dangers of smoking while it was taking huge financial contributions in the form of advertising from the tobacco industry. Before you accept information at face value, it is a good idea to know the back story of the source and how it relates to anyone's financial interests.

## Know Your Authorities and Their Prejudices

Who are the authorities we depend upon for our sources of learning and what are their prejudices, agendas, and intellectual blind spots? Most people rely upon their schools, religions, science and medicine, historians, parents, friends, the media, and government officials as their trusted authorities. Recently, I met with a college-educated Indonesian who told me with confidence that the reason the Muslim world has fallen so far behind the West is that "the Jews stole all of our technology." He had learned this in school and had no way to test that "fact" against reality. What about the members of the American Black community who have been told in their churches that the AIDS epidemic was designed by the white population and its government to wipe them out? Or what about the fundamentalist children who are being home-schooled by their parents to learn that the earth is only 6,000 years old? These may sound like extreme examples of misinformation, but remember that World War II landed unannounced on the unsuspecting European populations because their government officials and newspapers who maintained extreme pacifist leanings refused to believe and then report that the Germans were secretly using their factories to re-arm their military.

For traders, this principle of knowing your source and your source's prejudices and agendas is especially important. If you are basing your trading decisions on the writings and information from a particular market analyst, you need to know where he is coming from intellectually and emotionally. Is he bullish by nature? If so, he will filter out information that does not support his pre-conceived ideas.

### Be Skeptical

For example, just because you visit a foreign country and learn that its ordinary citizens are basically good people who only want to live in peace does not mean that its government feels kindly toward you and your country. Extrapolating from one experience can often mean that you are using the exception to make the rule. You may only be seeing a part of the picture, or you may not have the historical background and context into which to properly place your experience. Or you may be coming into a situation with a preconceived viewpoint (that you are not consciously aware of) that colors every piece of information you find, such as:

- The markets are bullish or bearish
- All people are good or bad
- Everything that is different from my culture is bad or good
- All historians are truthful or liars
- Life is full of tragedy and hopelessness or possibility and hope

Regardless of what you believe, your brain will filter the information you take in to support your belief and filter out or explain away the information that contradicts your beliefs. Since traders need to have their information in the unvarnished form, it is vital that they look beyond their own experience and emotions to learn what is really going on in the world.

Who knew that learning could become so complicated in its implications? Actually, every major government on earth knows this fact and most of them work hard to control the information that is available and taught in their schools. After World War II, Russia carefully rewrote history books in its schools and Japan expurgated its history books of any culpability. And in authoritarian countries and societies, students are taught, in addition, not to question authorities or to think or research the facts for themselves.

So, what does all of this have to do with trading and making money? Along with basic science, trading is one of the purest professions when it comes to searching for the truth. Yes, traders are swept away by emotion and caught up in herd thinking just like everyone else. But they do so at their peril. The market is either going up or down (or static), but wishing it to be different does not change the facts. A trader who can learn to learn without the baggage of his or anyone else's political, personal, or social agendas is going to come out on top.

## WHAT TO LEARN?

What to learn is, of course, just as important as how to learn.

1. **Trading issues:** A trader should devote a certain proportion of his learning to issues related directly to trading. For that reason, he should be reading every book on the subject that he can find. The more widely he reads, the less likely he will be to fall victim to the influence of any one voice or viewpoint, until he finds a voice he feels confidence in trusting to be as unbiased as possible. In addition, he would do well to read about the technical aspects of trading, the market both locally and globally, and trading psychology. He should be attending as many seminars, workshops, and trading conventions and symposiums as he can.
2. **Economics, political science, history:** But, then, he should be widening his grasp of the world of trading by throwing his net out further and further into the realms of general economics, political science, and history. The operation of markets is best understood in the light of historical perspective.
3. **Business issues:** In addition, a trading career is a business and a trader is an entrepreneur. For that reason, a trader who wants to be in business for a long time would do well to learn more about operating a business. Not only are there excellent books available about business management, most communities have a local business college or community college that offers courses on running a business, accounting principles, taxes, and personnel management.
4. **Health issues:** Then, too, a trader might well put some time into learning about health issues. As soon as a trader reaches his forties, his ability to prosper will have more and more to do each year with how healthy he is and how much energy he has to deal with the demands of trading. If he pays for his own insurance, he will want to maintain his health just to ensure that he can hold onto his insurance. Online information services abound that provide consumers with the latest research into health issues.
5. **Spiritual issues:** A trader's wellbeing is affected by more than just his physical and psychological health. His spiritual health is an issue that he might want to learn more about. Exploring his own spiritual and religious heritage is a place to start, but he might want to extend his exploration to other spiritual practices.
6. **Science and technology:** The history and current developments in science and technology are a source of great excitement. For example, the emerging sciences of bioinformatics (the application of vast computing power to solving biological problems such as pandemics) and biophotonics (the application of light technology to biology) are the future of both life and technology for us, with extraordinary opportunities for investment.

7. **Art, fiction, performance:** Learning should not end at that which you can reduce to logic and reality. Imagination extends the creative problem solving part of the human brain. There is much to learn about the human experience from learning how to sing and dance, how to play an instrument, how to act, how to write a piece of fiction, or how to paint a landscape.

## CONCLUSION

The point is that a trader's world needs to continue to expand if he is to maintain his skill as a successful trader. Developing the discipline of learning something every day will help him to keep his mind keen in order to be a better and better trader. But, a savvy trader must also take responsibility for the process of learning. Just like we now know that we have to read the labels before we toss something into our shopping carts and then pop it into our bodies, we have to read the labels before we willy-nilly accept everything that comes our way in the guise of truth and good information. Traders live and work in a highly complex world, in which only the most vigilant, disciplined, and intelligently skeptical will prosper.

*When you become too comfortable, you will not grow.*

CHAPTER 24

# Stretching Your Trading Discipline

Discipline is the most important part of being a successful trader! Anyone who has ever traded knows and understands the importance of this statement. Perhaps, some would argue that discipline is the most important factor after a winning strategy for entering and exiting trades has been found. However, I would point out that even the process of developing a trading system requires discipline.

Those of you who are already successful in the markets might not want to change anything that you are doing because you have found a combination that works for you. For those of you who feel this way, I would agree that you should keep doing what you are doing. But for those who are becoming bored or want to stretch your abilities and your profits, you might consider stretching your discipline.

To move to a new level of elevated performance in any endeavor takes stretching beyond your comfort zone. When you accomplish this, you are more likely to be able to reap the rewards of working at a higher level of skill.

Anyone who has participated in any form of athletics knows the importance of stretching to achieve higher performance. Without stretching, you will limit your ability to perform and perhaps even injure yourself. When I was a concert singer, I practiced singing to the F above High C so I could sing in a range to High C without straining my voice. As a dancer, I practiced doing five spins on one foot without stopping so I would feel comfortable performing at four.

Traders also need to stretch to keep their trading interesting and allow them to experience more opportunity. You will recognize that more opportunity presents itself when you stretch from your comfort zone. This is a function of directing the mind to expand itself. If you do not keep growing, then you may sabotage your efforts from sheer boredom.

## STRETCHING AS A TRADER

The following are examples of how to do so.

### Trade Only a Portion of an Eight-hour Day

Many traders remain attached to the old eight-hour workday ethic. One of the advantages that traders enjoy is that they do not have to work a full eight hours to receive the benefit of a full day's wage. I know a number of traders who make a very comfortable living from trading in one or two hours a day. In fact, I have suggested to several of the traders that I coach that they trade less hours. They have found that they earn more money and enjoy life and trading more because they are less stressed. Of course, this does not mean that you take away study time or development time, especially when you are a beginning trader.

Notice the patterns when you make and lose money. Try to recognize the time of day, time of week, time of year, and your personal energy during those times. This information should give you a clear picture of what times are best for you to earn the most profits.

### Take Larger Risks

A few traders have said to me, "I wish that I could feel comfortable trading more contracts." Let's assume that their comfort level is at 10 contracts and they want to trade 100 contracts. To jump from 10 contracts to 100 is too big of a stretch. But, trading 15 contracts on what you "intuit" to be the better trades would be a workable psychological stretch to start toward a new level of risk. When that level of risk becomes comfortable, you might be ready to stretch risk to 20 contracts and so on. If you cannot incrementally build on assuming more risk, then go back to what you are comfortable with and/or seek out coaching if you are not satisfied with what you are risking.

### Take More Trades

Some traders do not have the ability to trade all of the signals that their system gives. Like the previous suggestion of increasing risk, begin slowly by increasing the number of trades each day and reward yourself for your efforts. Most trading systems are designed to gain the most profit only if you take all of the signals. If this is the case with your system, and you have been unable to take your trades, still build slowly. Realize that you might not make profits during this time, but that you are building the discipline necessary to follow your system.

Too many traders become angry with themselves for not taking all of the trades from their system and it leads to their demise as a trader. When you enjoy the process of becoming more disciplined each day and know that you are drawing closer to your goal, you will be less likely to frustrate yourself into making bad choices. Most traders do not begin their trading career by making money. It is the way that the process of becoming a trader is handled that will determine whether or not you will be able to stay the course.

One of the ways to become more disciplined in following your rules is learning not to make the same mistakes over and over. If you are among the few traders who make profits from the beginning, be sure to develop contingency plans for the inevitable drawdown. Sometimes, it is better to experience loss from the beginning because it toughens you for times when a drawdown in equity occurs.

## Take Fewer Trades

Taking too many trades is usually more of a problem than not taking enough. If this is an issue for you, start to qualify your trades on a scale of 1 to 10 with 10 being best, and only take the better trades. When you qualify your trades, you will begin to notice more detail in the most profitable trades. Two options to qualify trades can be with a technical filtering system or by using some form of discretion. The important thing is to adjust your rules to any changes that are made, so you don't give the impression to your neurology that it is okay to go against your rules.

## Try Other Markets

For a change, you might test your system in other markets. If you have been consistently making money in one commodity and want to branch out to find more opportunities, you might begin testing your method on other commodities. Trade these markets only if you have tested your system and have determined that it is likely to bring in additional profits. If you find that this confuses you or does not work for some reason, then go back to your original method. Everyone has a different level of tolerance and focus. For some people, one market is all that they can handle, while others become bored and lose profits if they don't juggle trading several commodities.

## Monitor Other Methods

For those of you who love the research and development phase of trading, you might start developing other methods and monitor their progress while following your original method as long as it does not interfere with your performance. Trading two or more systems might be advantageous. The new system might work better when the markets change or you might find that you benefit just by keeping your creative juices flowing.

If you enjoy developing systems, there is also the possibility of selling systems that you have developed. Just make sure that you do not change your profit making system too frequently. A periodic review every three months is a good benchmark for reviewing and re-testing your system. You don't want to kill the golden goose.

## Listen to Talks and Read Books

One new idea can make a dramatic difference in your trading results. Always give yourself time in the day to study beyond what you already know. The more education you have, the more you will be able to recognize opportunity. I'm also not referring to education that directly relates to trading. Ask yourself before you embark on any new learning experience, "What does this have to do with trading and making money?" and notice the answer when it comes.

Of course, be cautious about letting other people's ideas confuse you. Give yourself permission to try out new ideas only when you are working on a periodic review of your system.

## Improve Your Tools and Environment

Remember your first computer? Remember how slow and limited in features it was when compared to the one that you are using now? Each year there is new technology and new tools that will enhance your performance. Make sure that you keep up to date with what is available. A good method for keeping up with technological advances is by going to trading conferences and reviewing trade magazines and publications

Occasionally, review your working environment and ask yourself how you can make it more conducive to nurturing top performance. Consider these possibilities:

- less clutter in your working environment
- a larger flat computer screen or a panel of screens
- a faster computer
- better software

- better lighting
- more efficient and/or less expensive services
- an assistant
- an ergonomic chair

### Self-Improvement

After you have been trading for a time, you will begin to realize that trading is a trip of self-discovery. Many traders find that discovering themselves is more important than making money. But usually, you don't begin to think this way until you are earning money consistently. When you add new skills, abilities, and education to your resources, you build your self-worth and when traders feel good about themselves, their trading improves.

## CONCLUSION

The type of person who becomes a successful trader is usually a multifaceted individual who needs constant stimulation. For this reason, stretching from the normal range of one's ability and focus should be an important part of a successful trader's life. Earning profits is usually the goal of every trader, but when you add to that goal "enjoying the process of earning profits," it is more likely that you will earn more profits and have a better life.

---

*Bigger is not necessarily better and smaller may not be enough.*

---

CHAPTER 25

# Thinking Large for Traders

Should traders set large goals that seem impossible to achieve or should they set smaller, more realistic ones? Should they try to tackle all of their goals at once or just one at a time? Which strategies produce better results? The answers may surprise you.

## REALISTIC THINKING

Realists tend to win arguments. They use facts and figures, logic, and common sense to bolster their positions. On paper, everything presented by the realist looks much better than the positions held by the unrealistic dreamer. Realists rarely get themselves into trouble and they create stability in their environments. In fact, the world needs realistic thinkers to keep the rest of us from drifting off into the stratosphere. They keep the uninformed and the lazy honest by testing their positions against the facts. This all sounds good, so what is the problem?

Years ago, while I was conducting research into the lives of highly successful people, I interviewed a man who was a real estate mogul long before real estate became the hyped-up source of speculation for the Johnny-come-latelies. I asked him his secret for success and he said he could sum it up in one phrase. "I was too stupid to know what you couldn't do," he said with a wink. Then, he proceeded to tell me that he would walk into a deal with lawyers who would explain in detail why it was unrealistic and could not work. He said that, in his experience, lawyers were trained to find the problems in a situation and not the opportunities. In fact, for him, they epitomized the realistic thinker.

Our real estate mogul was convinced that you could not make real money if you thought realistically. This is also true for those who want to lose weight. People who set realistic goals are not as likely to lose as much weight as those who set unrealistic goals. I have experienced this myself and have seen that this was also true for many of my friends when I was a model. For years, dieters have been cautioned to set the most realistic goals. In fact, if you look at major weight-loss programs such as Weight Watchers, dieters are advised to set only the most modest of goals—a pound or two a week. One factor for those who lose more weight when they have unrealistic expectations, is that they are motivated by their optimistic expectations. Traders must constantly guard against the misperceptions of their families and close friends that they do not deal in the real world and that they are pie-in-the-sky dreamers who should get "real" jobs. When these types of so-called unrealistic traders succeed, they are able to succeed on a much greater scale than those who have set their goals realistically.

## THE ONE-GOAL-AT-A-TIME STRATEGY

Here is the second element of realistic thinking: If you have a set of goals, it is best to address one goal at a time rather than attempt to do them all at once. The logic here is that you will make steady and slow progress toward the completion of each and every goal, given sufficient time. The concern is that if you attempt to address all of your goals simultaneously, you will be overwhelmed by so much change and so much challenge that you will lose focus and concentration, and give up the effort entirely.

This one-goal-at-a-time process is just another variation of the one-toe-into-the-water-at-a-time method that gets you into the pool very, very gradually, rather than diving in all at once. If you take it slowly into the pool, your body will slowly adjust to the cold water rather than being hit with the shock of the cold all at once. So, which one are you—the one who takes it slowly into the pool or the one who plunges in? If you are the one who takes it an inch at a time, have you noticed that your friend who plunged in is swimming around and enjoying the pool while you are still working on getting your arms wet?

Could it be that combining goals gives you more motivation to succeed than if you take it just one step at a time? Is the sum total of progress along a number of fronts so much greater than the progress you can see on one front that you are inspired to keep going? If the question is total momentum, than you can add even more goals into the mix. Why stop at just a few?

## OPTIMISM VS. PESSIMISM

Setting large goals appears to require more optimism in the outcome than the realistic thinker who sets realistic goals. Realistic thinkers tend to be more pessimistic in my experience than the thinking large individuals. If a trader tends to be a pessimist, he will also tend to set smaller, more realistic goals. But, this type of thinking may significantly reduce his ultimate level of achievement.

It would be a social scientist's dream to get a thousand traders who were realistic thinkers (i.e., pessimistic thinkers) to set unrealistic goals and compare the results to an equal number of control subjects who are also realistic thinkers who would set realistic goals. Would the first group of traders do significantly better than the control group? I believe they would.

## THINKING LARGE EXERCISES

With all of the social and political pressures on a trader to be realistic thinkers, especially in view of the current economic situation, it is important to stay aware of the implications of these two studies. Realistic thinking is small thinking and small thinking creates small results. Unrealistic thinking is optimistic thinking, and it is demonstrated in these studies that this kind of thinking creates large results—the kind of thinking that a trader with ambition to succeed must cultivate. So, here are some exercises and strategies to keep your thinking large and, by extension, your results as well.

### Goal Setting

If you have not done a goal-setting exercise in recent time, set aside some time. But, do not think of this process as a chore or as something that would be other than pleasant. For this goal-setting exercise to be effective, it should be framed as a truly enjoyable experience, like getting a massage or being treated to a great meal. The reason for setting the atmosphere for this goal-setting experience as a relaxing, delightfully rewarding experience is because you cannot set large goals if you are worried or anxious, depressed, feeling tight and stressed, or reluctant. This goal-setting exercise is designed to get you dreaming of what you would really want. Thus, you cannot be constrained by the superego voice in your head that tells you that your goal is unrealistic, unnecessary, over-the-top, greedy, self-indulgent, or that you do not deserve it for any number of reasons.

The best goal-setting experience I ever had was at the side of a beautiful Olympic-sized pool, while I was lying on a chaise lounge under a brilliant cloudless sky on a warm summer day. With no one to bother me, I filled two pages of a yellow legal pad with the most impossible goals I could imagine. Five years later, I found that list and, to my astonishment, I had fulfilled each and every one of those impossible goals. I had thought large and had been rewarded.

So, when you do this thinking large goal setting, you want to plant yourself in a place where you can dream really big. I recommend being somewhere around water or nature—a place where you are in touch with the sky and the vastness of things. You want to make certain that you will not be interrupted by anyone, so do not bring your cell phone with you.

Now, start to write. What are the biggest goals you have—the long-term ones and the short-term ones? What are the impossible and unrealistic ones? Do not allow yourself to be censored. No one is watching you and no one cares. It turns out that the only one who limits the size of your goals is you. But a caveat here: No one is looking over your shoulder as you create these goals, and you should keep it that way. Your goals are your business and no one else's. The larger the goals, the more others will be threatened by them and will want to sabotage them by eroding your confidence and ridiculing you for entertaining such lofty goals.

### The Plan

Once you have written down your large, unrealistic goals, you will need to do some planning. Here is where it is possible and even positive to include some realistic thinking. You will want to take stock of your assets and resources so that you can mobilize them to help you achieve your goals. You will want to make use of every one of these resources, and especially all of your personal contacts. We often achieve our most impossible goals through a serendipitous chain of personal contacts that bring us to the exact person required to make our impossible goal a reality. It is helpful to make lists of the steps you will need to take to reach your goals and the people you will need to contact. And this is the part that goes against conventional wisdom: Work on these goals simultaneously, and not sequentially.

### The Rewards

I have learned to reward each success and each step achieved on the path to a goal as a way of reinforcing future successes. If you have been thinking large and setting large goals, when you achieve them, you will need to reward yourself large as well. Small rewards for the achievement of large goals defeats the process by sending the wrong message to your neurology. So, in your planning, you might also want to list the rewards you would like to give yourself for achieving these goals. Make those rewards so enticing that you become overwhelmed with excitement at the thought.

## CONCLUSION

Large results do not come from thinking small. If you want to be a highly successful trader, you will need to nurture your ability to think large, to be optimistic in your goals, and to aim with a shotgun to achieve them rather than a rifle. To think large, you will have to leave behind the limiting realistic thinking that supports a pessimistic view of what can be achieved and how long it will take.

---

*Play in the field of dreams of what seems to be impossible, and you might find out it is possible just by allowing the dream to be there.*

---

CHAPTER 26

# Trading the Dream

If dreams are the gallant steeds upon which traders triumphantly enter the Kingdom of Market Success, then fantasies are the shimmering illusions set in their path to defeat them. It is vital for traders to know the difference.

Fantasy is an important part of childhood. Do you remember how, as a child, you wanted to be a cowboy or, perhaps, a super hero? You rode around the house on your broomstick pony, only to be disillusioned by your older brother telling you to sweep the floor. Perhaps, you wore that cape made out of an old towel, knowing that you could leap tall buildings at a single bound, only to find yourself with a broken arm when you jumped out of your first-story window. Now, all grown up, you have a new fantasy to be a commodity trader and to reap all the rewards and adulations that come from being successful, only to find that you have lost your bank account along with the fantasy.

## DREAMS DO COME TRUE

The words dream and fantasy are often used as synonyms, but the difference between them is far greater than semantics. These two words represent two opposing philosophical positions. A dream, though not yet a reality, has the potential to become one. A dream is created in order to manifest a future reality. Dreams represent intention.

A young athlete who dreams of becoming an Olympic gold-medal winner is the young man or woman who then practices eight hours a day, makes sacrifices of time, effort, comfort, and immediate gratification. The traders who dream of becoming great traders arise early to start the day, spend countless hours reading about their field, then research, develop, and test their methodologies and systems, and take every opportunity to develop themselves psychologically and professionally.

It is true that many dreams appear, on the surface, to be as impossible to turn into reality as fantasies. So, what separates a dream from a fantasy? **A dream is a fantasy that you really want to make happen.**

A dream represents something that you really care about, something that makes you want to take action to turn it into reality. A dream is a true motivating force and the making of it into a reality becomes a need.

Dreams often start out as visions without form and detail, just like most fantasies. But, once you see the vision as a real goal, it takes on the form of a dream in which you begin to give it shape and detail. As it develops, you add color, texture, sound, smell, and emotion to it. The more of these elements you add to the original vision, the more of a dream it becomes. When the dream is dreamed with passion and frequency, even when you are dreaming what seems to be an impossible dream, you are more likely to make it a reality. Difficulties and challenges become part of an experiential process in making that dream come true when it is a dream you really want to happen, with everything that comes with it becoming real.

## FANTASIES

Fantasies, however, are not necessarily something we want to experience in reality. While a fantasy might have the same appearance as a dream, its manifestation would not necessarily be something that would please you. For example, you might fantasize about the death of someone at whom you are angry, but, hopefully, you would not really want that fantasy to become a reality. It is common for people to have sexual fantasies that are pleasurable in their non-reality form but not necessarily pleasurable in their actual realization. Many people fantasize about exciting and dangerous careers such as astronauts, firefighters, jet pilots, and spies that they would have no real interest in pursuing in reality.

Frequently, however, people fool themselves into believing that their fantasies are actually dreams or they cannot tell the difference between a particular fantasy and a dream. There are compelling reasons why this self-delusion occurs.

## The Fantasy Is a Realizable Goal

When a fantasy is not a realizable goal, there is no confusion: For example, a short, elderly woman who is a hundred pounds over-weight can fantasize about being a supermodel, but she knows that it is simply a fantasy. However, when a tall and slender young woman fantasizes about being a supermodel, she may begin to believe that her fantasy has air under its wings. It is clear that the fantasy of becoming a dragon slayer is a not a realizable goal. But, many fantasies are within the bounds of reason. Thus, an intelligent and highly trained individual with a good track record of self-discipline and accomplishments can tell himself that his fantasy of becoming a top trader is real, since he possesses the prerequisite assets and resources.

## Others Have Achieved the Fantasy

When the successes of highly motivated dreamers achieving their impossible dreams are widely advertised, it is easy for others to see their same fantasies as dreams: For example, the stories of Thomas Edison finding the secret to making a light bulb after 40,000 failures, of Michael Jordan becoming the greatest basketball player on earth after being rejected by his varsity basketball team, of Abe Lincoln becoming president of the United States after being born in a log cabin, of Aristotle Onassis becoming one of the richest men on earth after a childhood of poverty. The list is long enough to include virtually every field of endeavor. Thus, anyone who considers a fantasy of becoming a fabulously wealthy trader can find an example of his fantasy having become a reality for someone else.

## Others Are Cheering You On

If you tell supportive, visionary people in your life about your fantasy, you might be surprised to discover that they believe you are not only committed to turning it into a reality but that you are capable of doing so. These believers may unwittingly become your cheerleaders in a cause which you have no genuine intention of following to completion. Unfortunately, you might begin to believe the hype that accompanies your words, finding yourself in the unintended role of turning your fantasy into a reality. This situation is the sorry fate of individuals who vocalize their fantasy to run for elected office only to find themselves in a race for a seat they do not really want to occupy. It is also the story of unintended weddings, families, and assignments.

## TELLING FANTASIES FROM DREAMS

How can you tell if your fantasy is just that and not a real dream? Actually, it is relatively easy to distinguish between a fantasy and a dream by taking the following test. You can write down your answers or merely verbalize them to yourself. The only requirement is being totally honest with yourself.

### Describe Your Fantasy

Look at your fantasy and describe it in detail. Talk about what you see and hear and feel and taste. Relate as much particularity as possible.

- What does it look like?
- What emotions are you feeling?
- What are you doing in your fantasy?
- What are the rewards of your fantasy?
- What are the consequences of your fantasy?

### Assess Its Intensity

How detailed is this fantasy?

- What is the nature of your emotions?
- How intense are these emotions?
- What would you gain or lose by this fantasy becoming a reality?

### Assess Your Commitment

What is required to turn this fantasy into reality and am I willing to do it?

- What are you not willing to do to turn this into a reality?
- How much time, effort, and money are you willing to put into it?
- How much pain and loss are you willing to bear?
- How much rejection and failure and embarrassment are you willing to tolerate to reach this goal?
- How long are you willing to go the distance?

### Assess Your Need

How much do you need to reach this goal and how will you feel about yourself and your life if you do not achieve this goal?

### Assess Its Reality Quotient

Is this goal achievable?

- Have others achieved this goal?
- Have others with your assets and resources achieved this goal?
- Are you willing to make your fantasy public to family, friends, and associates?
- Will the significant people in your life support you in achieving this goal?
- And how will you be affected if they tell you it is hopeless and impossible?

Now that you have honestly examined your fantasy, you will be able to determine if you have a level of emotional need and commitment sufficient to bring it to fruition. If you do, then what you have is really a dream, a realizable dream that has legs on which to travel.

If you discover that your dream is meaningful to you, the act of describing it in detail and giving it sensory aspects will actually help you to turn that dream into reality. When people who have achieved their impossible dreams tell you that they could actually taste their victory, could hear the crowds roaring, could feel the sweat on their brow, you know that they were living their dreams before they actually achieved them. This powerfully detailed visionary experience gives your neurology the plan as well as the motivation to reach your goal.

On the other hand, you can put aside your fantasy as merely entertainment and wishful thinking if:

- your ability to see and feel and taste your fantasy is anemic
- your willingness to experience the hardship and commitment its achievement will require is not powerful
- you are unwilling to take the actions that are required to turn this dream into reality

## CONCLUSION

Many traders come into the profession of trading under the spell of a fantasy. They have a vague idea of how successful they are going to be and how easy it is going to be for them. These traders are destined to fail. However, the traders who enter the field on the wings of a powerful dream are compelled to do whatever it takes to succeed, and succeed they will. It is important, therefore, to understand if you are a dreaming visionary or a wishful fantasizer.

---

*You will only be ready for the next level of success when you can follow your rules without question.*

---

CHAPTER 27

# Stretching Life to the Next Level of Success

Our neurological system is comfortable with our habitual behavior patterns and will support us with that status quo. I developed a Trader Evaluation to give feedback to traders so that they will know what is holding them back from achieving each next level of success. If you are losing, winning, or leveled out with consistent profits but not growing, you are very likely to stay in that situation unless you are willing to do what is necessary to stretch. Most people who want to increase their performance are willing to read a book or go to a seminar, but not willing to consistently follow through on what they have learned over the long haul. The question is, what does it take to stretch, and are you seriously willing to make that commitment? If you are not, then expect the same results. If you are, then get ready to take a trip to the next level of success. *My Trader Evaluation*, which is part of the *Trading on Target Home Study Course*, is a good first step in the process because through my evaluation I can tell you what is holding you back from top performance.

## REACH THE NEXT LEVEL OF SUCCESS IN TRADING

The fact is most of you have been high achievers in your life. But now that you have reached and perhaps maintained a level of success in your trading over a period of time are you willing to do what it takes to reach your next level of success? Most people are not, because they are comfortable with the status quo, they don't want to take on any additional risk or responsibility, or they are too lazy to do what is necessary to add new resources.

I was working with a floor trader named Bill. He was afraid of electronic trading, but knew that if he did not start to transition off the floor he would not be able to maintain his present lifestyle. His monthly bills were $15,000. With his wife enjoying her country clubs and charity work and his three children in private schools, he felt a tremendous pressure to do something fast.

Bill was a guy with a raspy voice and a limited vocabulary. He was raised in a rough neighborhood in the Bronx. His two older brothers had blue-collar jobs and so did all of his cousins. In fact, he was the only one of his friends that was able to rise out of a limiting mentality and rise to the top of the financial world. He left school in the tenth grade, but managed later to get a high school degree. One day a professional basketball player who he was shooting hoops with made him dream beyond the projects. He introduced Bill to a friend who was a trader and that introduction led to an opportunity in the markets. Bill became a runner at the New York Mercantile Exchange. From there it took him 20 years to become one of the best traders in the pit. He literally failed his way to success.

He came to one of the workshops that I was presenting at a conference. He confided to me about his fear of the future. Fortunately, his son taught him how to use the computer and he had read enough books on trading and technical analysis to give him a base to start in electronic trading. Bill said that he knew he could make money, but was afraid he would not be able to make the same kind of money that he was used to.

We started by eliminating the issues and the conflicts in his life that would keep him from believing that he wasn't capable of mastering electronic trading. Then I worked with him on the following model. These are the 10 steps to achieve the next level of success.

1. Focus on what you specifically want. In his case he knew that he wanted to trade the same commodity in the same time frame.
2. Plan how to achieve it.
   - **Resources—skills, abilities, education.** He needed additional information on how to build the technical part of trading, so I introduced him to a trading coach.
   - **Time, energy, money, risk.** In Bill's case the money and risk were not an issue but the energy and time was. I worked with him on how to increase his energy. He was going to have to trade less on the floor for a while, so we worked on him making more in less time.
   - **Contingencies.** Bill's biggest fear was that he would have to trade full-time electronically before he was ready. I made him realize that

he had been in training all of his trading life and just had to know how to transfer his training. Listing everything that could go wrong and right with the best possible outcome increased his confidence for the future.

- **Specific goals—tasks and time frame.** Bill was a goal setter, but found that writing them down with specific time limits made his way easier.
- **Who will be affected, and is it worth the price of how it will affect them?** This part was the most difficult. Bill's family was used to seeing a lot of him in the evenings. He sat his family down and asked for their support and he got it. But this didn't mean that he did not have a difficult time missing the family part of his life.
- **Consider how your life will change after you achieve your new level of success.** Will you be able to handle the new responsibilities and the new challenges as a result of attaining this stretch? In Bill's case he learned to trade with more risk and less time on the floor. This gave him more time for working behind the computer. He loved the fact that he finally felt smart. Even with all the money he earned, he never felt that way before.
- **Will you leave enough room for your creative process to flourish?** The process of working with Bill to become successful at electronic trading took almost a year. I felt that it was important that he did not exhaust himself as so many traders do when they try to make this transition. He was able to utilize his energy wisely, so his intuitive skills would work both on and off the floor.

3. Write an overview of your life's commitments and what you are willing to change, give up, or delegate to make your new level of success attainable.

   In this area, I made sure that Bill would use his time effectively by hiring the best people along the way so he could enjoy his transition more in the shortest amount of time. Bill's life was full before having to commit the time to learning a new way of trading, but his passion and need were greater. We just had to eliminate the fear for this passion to motivate him to achieve his goal.

4. It is important to have the significant people in your life be on board to support you in the changes you will make that affect them.

   While his family said that they would be supportive there were many disappointments along the way with each of them when he was not able to do the things they used to enjoy as a family.

5. Mentally rehearse the actions you will have to take in order for your neurological system to support you in these changes. See yourself enjoying the process.

Bill told me that mentally rehearsing himself already achieving his goal was the main thing that kept him going when the going got rough.

6. Intentionally direct your thoughts during the day and your dreams at night on your goal to create the passion necessary to get you through the more challenging days.

   Bill's dream is what helped his family to continue to support him.

7. Do what is necessary to create more vital energy, so that you will be able to handle the added stress.

   All along the way Bill learned that everything he took into his body, mind, and spirit was measured and directed for him to be the ultimate energy machine.

8. Align with people who are willing and enjoy assisting you.

   While Bill always felt the competition between other traders, he finally learned that there are many people who enjoy giving and sharing. He knows now that having people assist him made his way easier and more enjoyable.

9. Reward yourself along the way.

   Bill's reward before I started working with him was always about providing the best life for his family. He finally learned that he had rewards that he could enjoy just for himself, such as connecting with old friends and doing charity work with children.

10. Be a better person.

    While Bill was always ready to share in his personal life, he now finds it enjoyable to help other traders who are going through the same struggles he went through.

Now, I want to ask the question again. How many of you are willing to do what is necessary to get to the next level of success? If you are not, then enjoy what you have, if you are, then start now.

---

*When you start from a model of success, the path of success has less hurdles.*

---

CHAPTER 28

# The Happy Monkey

For two years, Rex worked hard to create a nearly perfect trading system. Once he was finally satisfied with his system, he paper traded it for another year until it was making very healthy profits on paper. When he was comfortable with the final adjustments he had made to his system, Rex was finally ready to risk his assets. Six months into his trading, he was receiving the financial rewards of the system that he had worked so diligently on. Two months later, he was second-guessing his system and losing money. What happened?

Rex was a very intelligent man with a lot of education and training in a technical field. He had always taken pride in his intelligence and his professional achievements. While Rex loved doing his market research and learning how to trade, his favorite part of trading was the development of his system. With his aptitude for learning and his advanced schooling, he was well suited for the preparation phase of his trading career. However, he was not prepared to trade every day. Rex thought he wanted to be a trader. But, in reality, he wanted to be a perpetual system developer. After six months of actual profitable trading, Rex was bored.

"I feel like a mindless monkey," he lamented, "who simply pulls the lever when the signal tells him to pull it. Is this all there is to trading?"

## THE BOREDOM CRISIS

If you have been trading for any length of time, you have encountered the Boredom Crisis experienced by Rex. For a successful trader, who has developed a working and profitable system, boredom can easily become the most serious problem that is faced. If a trader is to survive the boredom crisis, he must find answers that work to the following questions:

- How do you keep enjoying your trading when it becomes routine and predictable?
- When boredom sets in, how do you continue to follow your rules?
- How can you keep from sabotaging your trading in order to bring passion and excitement back to your professional life?

## THE TINKER TRADER

The average person who becomes a trader is anything but average. People who are attracted to trading are often highly motivated to be successful and to work hard. Traders tend to be interested in technology, mathematics, science, and economics. They frequently have more energy, more drive, and more ambition than the average person. And because the average trader tends to be far more intelligent and better educated than the average person, he requires intellectual challenges and stimulation to keep him interested in what he is doing.

That need for intellectual challenge and stimulation is what often gets good traders into trouble.

Highly educated people are trained to think, to look for problems, and find their solutions by questioning, improving, and changing. When these individuals become traders, they are turned on by the challenge of learning how the markets work. They read everything they can find about trading. They attend seminars and immerse themselves in their research. They love the stimulation of developing a trading system and testing it until it is highly effective. They like to learn and love to keep improving upon perfection. In short, they love to tinker. These thinkers become part of the great tinkering class and when they move into the trading profession, they become tinker traders, fiddling with their systems and always trying to make them better.

## THE TRADER SHARK

So, what is wrong with being a tinker, especially for a trader? After all, is it not a good thing for a trader to be constantly finding ways to improve his trading? The short answer is a qualified maybe. It depends on what he is doing and why. If he is in the development phase of his trading, tinkering is a positive as he makes a good system better. But, if a trader is actually trading, tinkering with a system is the perfect example of the saying: "Don't fix it if it ain't broke!" Unfortunately, someone who tinkers often does so because he feels the need.

A serious problem arises for a tinker trader when he is not fixing, fiddling, or improving. He is unhappy and becomes bored. Just as a shark must keep moving through the water to live, a tinker trader becomes bored if he is not adding value to what he does in his daily life. Boredom for a tinker trader is a form of death. In order to feel alive again, he must start to move once more. That movement for a trader involves getting back into the game of challenging his mind with tinkering. So, he starts to change his system and second guessing it until he finally creates enough havoc in his trading that he has to start all over again. In the wake of all this destruction, he gets to feel the challenge that he misses in his boring, predictable but highly profitable trading.

## THE SELF-ESTEEM FACTOR

The boredom problem for the intelligent trader is complicated by an additional factor. Most educated people are conditioned to link their self-esteem to their intelligence, and not just their passive intelligence but to their active intelligence. So, if a trader with this background is not actively using his intelligence to tinker, he begins to lose his sense of self-worth. In fact, since he probably defines himself through his intelligence, his sense of who he is and what he has to contribute will suffer when he feels that he is not using his intelligence.

Self-esteem is a necessary ingredient for successful trading because it is the basis for self-confidence. Traders need self-confidence to stay disciplined and focused as they trade and they need confidence to handle the losses that are built into their trading system. So, when a tinker trader stops tinkering, not only does he get bored, he begins to sabotage his system and stops trading well because he loses confidence.

So, what is a bored and unhappy tinker trader to do?

## THE HAPPY MONKEY

Traders have a lot in common with athletes. The great challenge for a former athlete is to give up competition when he is no longer able to compete. Some retired athletes become so bored and despondent that they take up drugs and alcohol or other self-destructive activities. Their sense of self is so invested in their physicality that they feel worthless when they no longer have the speed, endurance, and strength that they once had.

While some retired athletes self-destruct, others find ways to constructively channel their skills successfully into a new arena. One way is for them to coach other athletes, using their experience on the playing field. Another way is to use their competitive instincts to succeed in business, sales, or another field where a high level of motivation is an important attribute. Some even retrain for entirely new careers and then use the personal skills they honed as athletes to succeed in their new field.

Using the retired athlete analogy, traders can find constructive ways to re-channel their need to tinker that does not interfere with their trading. For example, tinker traders can:

- Always be working on an alternative system
- Hire someone to trade their system while they work on a new one
- Find a completely new outlet outside of trading to satisfy their need to tinker and be intellectually challenged—such as designing a computer program, taking a course in advanced math, or learning a new language

## BECOMING THE HAPPY MONKEY

An alternative to re-channeling your need to tinker is to become the happy monkey, rather than the unhappy monkey. I proposed this choice to our self-sabotaging trader, Rex. In his mind, Rex had the image of himself as a person who needed to be improving something in order to be happy. What I had Rex do was to create a new image of himself in his mind.

The new picture was of a person who had accomplished the tinkering in the past, but now had permission to follow his rules. This picture comes with the understanding that there is a prize out there for following his rules. That prize is that he will be the person who adds value when he has mastered his technique and can use his intuition as a new filter. Having permission to use intuition in his trading is a treasure, indeed, because it allows Rex the ability to use his mind again in a way that is constantly challenging and new each time. However, he cannot use the intuition filter unless he has mastered his technique and mastered his own psychology.

When Rex became bored following his trading rules, he began to anticipate signals or second guess them. As a result, he entered trades too soon, got out of them too soon, and, generally, mucked up his trading system. A system that was making a certain amount of money was suddenly only achieving half of that return. Once Rex saw himself in a different light, as a person who had already done the necessary tinkering, but who had permission to follow his rules so that he could get a great reward, he began to follow his rules again. Then, the reinforcement of his good behavior was the reward that he could use his intuitive signals to trade. Suddenly, trading became challenging again. The unhappy monkey had become the happy monkey. Incidentally, Rex's system is now making even more money than before he reached the boredom crisis.

Another suggestion I gave Rex was to take a piece of graph paper with large boxes and make a square so that he would have the equivalent of approximately the number of trades he would take in two months. Then, I had him draw a line down the square from top to bottom with each section representing the percentage of estimated wins and losses based on past performance. His job as a trader was to follow his rules and fill in the boxes with a "W" or an "L" representing winning and losing trades. If he did his job by following his rules and putting a representation of a win or loss in each box, he would have a visual representation of what was needed for an overall profit.

When a trader has completed the square and can honestly say that he took all of the trades, then he will know that he is psychologically ready to go to the next level of monitoring an intuitive filter on top of his technique. If he has not been able to do this, it is time to consider the possibility of a trader's coach or trading coach depending upon whether it is the system or the trader that is not working.

## CONCLUSION

Boredom is inevitable for traders who have been trained to think and to tinker until something is perfect when they find themselves locked into trading a system and following its rules. Tinkering with something that works typically produces a string of losses. For many traders, a good alternative to becoming an unhappy, bored monkey can be found in the process of redirecting the energy into something that uses it constructively. An even better solution is to create a new internal model that redefines your role, your goals, and your rewards. This new self-image allows a trader to feel good about following his rules, while allowing him to be challenged by adding an intuitive signal. The result is a happy monkey and a successful trader.

---

*Paying the price in the beginning for what you need to be successful is less costly than paying it after you have failed.*

---

CHAPTER 29

# Shrinking from Opportunity

Opportunity is all around us. True, there are occasions when it is challenging to locate it when conditions have changed or the supply has temporarily shrunk and the competition for finite resources has dramatically increased. But, even in the worst of circumstances, opportunity is always there to be found. Since a trader's success depends upon finding opportunities and maximizing them, the problem is serious if he or she loses the ability to identify and pursue opportunity.

As time passes, traders often shrink from opportunity. The main reason is that people tend to dislike change. When we are younger, change is frequently linked to fun, excitement, and reward. However, over time, we eventually experience enough pain through change that we come to associate change with pain rather than opportunity. As we age, our brain works harder to keep us in an increasingly smaller comfort zone while protecting us from change and the possible opportunities and/or pain that come with it.

## THE PARADOX

To be successful, a trader must create patterns that are reproducible. These patterns need to become so familiar that they can be followed automatically. Just like everyone else who is human, a trader does this because our neurology is comfortable with patterns. We unconsciously reproduce patterns all day long: We blink our eyes, our hearts beat, our arms swing in opposition to our feet when we walk, our bodies move according to predictable patterns, and so on. These patterns allow us to feel normal and that everything is okay.

For a trader to be successful, he must also create in his existence ongoing patterns of behavior and thinking that are unconscious. The problem for traders is that they also have a built-in conflict or paradox. Within their routine, they must also have the kind of flexible thinking that allows them to adjust to subtle changes in the marketplace and fluctuating conditions while seeing opportunities that others miss. If this kind of flexibility does not co-exist with an ongoing routine, the markets will leave a trader behind.

## CREATING A BALANCE

To make this paradox work, it is necessary to create a balance between the opposing forces of routine and flexibility. The best way to accomplish this is to make conscious choices in your life that expand into areas that are outside of your trading. For example:

- Order new things from the menu or eat new types of food
- Take a trip to a city or country that you have never visited
- Read new materials—novels if you read non-fiction or subjects that you may have never considered like history or philosophy
- Listen to music that you do not ordinarily listen to—jazz, classical, opera, New Age, Indian music
- Attend a meeting that represents people with whom you don't normally associate
- Take courses in fields of study that are not associated with work—art classes, courses in science or law
- Attend worship services with a different religion or sect
- Volunteer to work with handicapped, disadvantaged, sick, or elderly people
- Join a task force or a volunteer rescue squad

Any new activity or challenge that stretches your imagination opens new perspectives that will help create the kind of versatility in your thinking that will allow you to maintain that fragile but ever-important balance in your thinking.

## BORED IN TRADING

Traders get trapped in their patterns because they become comfortable. The old patterns can be ill fitting and lead to terminal boredom, but traders find these discomforts acceptable because they are a part of a pattern that is safe, predictable, and sure. It is really frightening to expand beyond a pattern because a new discomfort may be even more uncomfortable than the old ones.

If a trader finds that he must stay in his comfort zone of predictable patterns to keep his trading rules, he must also become aware of other markets and anything new that is happening educationally. If not, his trading routine will become monotonous and predictable. At first, the routine of trading was exciting because the trading itself was exciting. Now, the activity has become so routine that the emotions and feelings that previously made trading a passion are no longer present. Without the good feelings, a trader has a tendency to sabotage his trading by creating excitement through accepting increased risk.

## GETTING BACK THAT OLD FEELING

Trading becomes a joy for successful traders because of the good feelings created in the beginning: The satisfaction of becoming a trader who had mastered the subject, created the trading rules, and learned to be disciplined. These positive feelings were an essential part of the original pattern. Ironically, the one pattern that most traders eventually force out of their routine is that good feeling. Sometimes, the pattern will change when a trader is in it, just like a physical phenomenon will change when it is observed. Ironically, the only way to retain the pattern of good feelings in your trading is to continue to do the same things that created the pattern originally. In other words, you must build change into the pattern. You must continue to:

- Conduct periodic reviews to improve your trading rules
- Develop and expand your mental and psychological capacities
- Continue to study the markets and perhaps develop new systems

The experience of regaining the good feelings from an old pattern can be compared to riding a bicycle. In order to ride it, you had to learn to balance. You struggled with the process until you finally understood and mastered it. Once you were successful, you were filled with an overwhelming sense of accomplishment and satisfaction. As you pedaled, you were looking at the ground and everything around you with a new sense of appreciation, excitement, and empowerment. Suddenly, you approached the lake and saw it as if for the first time. You were filled with all the good feelings that come from the newness of the experience. But then, time passes.

You have long since mastered balancing on your bike and have ridden it every day for years. The newness becomes sameness. At a point, you stop seeing the lake and the beauty surrounding it. You stop recognizing the routine. The experience of riding the bicycle becomes the big picture instead of the intimate details. It is the details that create the feelings of joy, satisfaction, excitement, and anticipation.

The same principle applies to trading. If you want to create the good feelings that come from being a good trader, you must work on the process of trading and create the pattern of detail that supports you being a good trader and following your rules. Like riding your bike, once you create the pattern of following your rules, you have the pattern of the details. Without revitalizing the pattern with the details that create good feelings, you are left with the part of you that will want to sabotage your rules to get those feelings back.

## THE DOOR TO OPPORTUNITY

When you are following your trading rules, you will have days when you simply know that certain trades are better than others. You develop this knowingness over time from experience in the markets and from your methodology. This knowingness is the key to opening the door to greater opportunity. This is your intuitive indicator, which does not replace your technical indicators. It gives you an additional indicator that is very powerful.

If trading becomes so routine that you no longer feel excitement for the routine itself, you will miss seeing various possibilities within each opportunity. You will be biking down the same old path, unable to see the lake and the details of the scene before you. However, if you are constantly reinventing your trading within the routine to keep up the good feelings, you will know when that shade becomes lighter or darker and you will be able to distinguish the opportunities from the potholes.

## STOPPED AT THE DOOR

The people who once traded on the floors of the Exchanges were excited about trading. Yes, they had the same-old, same-old routine to follow, and they had to deal with the damage to their voices and health. But, the excitement of the trading itself was always present. Then, the pits changed and the quality of that experience also changed. Many traders held onto what once was and did not adjust to what now is. They attempted to attach the old thrill of the winner to a diminishing number of contracts. Their long-established trading patterns required them to trade a certain number of contracts and take a certain amount of risk in order to feel the feelings and enjoy the process. They were still trying to make the trades happen when the opportunities were no longer there and they were not flexible enough to adjust to their new environment. These old floor traders eventually began taking significant losses.

The problems multiplied for these traders when they started trying to work their old trading systems within the new markets. The new methods of trading were very boring to them. They could no longer reproduce the good feelings through the pattern of details in their trading routines. Instead the only way to reproduce those good feelings with the excitement for trading was through accepting larger and larger risks.

In the beginning of their trading careers, the veteran floor traders may have started by taking on 10 contracts at a time. As they built their portfolios, they may have taken on 300 contracts at a time within normal risk parameters. Under the new system, they were forced back to the level of 30 to 40 contracts and could no longer experience the same thrill they had felt when they had originally raised themselves to that level. This process of attenuation is very much like the process of becoming hooked on addictive drugs. The rush on the way up to larger doses cannot be re-experienced on the way up the second time because the nervous system is already set to release those pleasure-creating beta endorphins at a much higher level.

So, in defeat, they left the trading floor and tried to trade on computers using their old embedded sensory-based inputs—the roar of the crowd, the taste of the grease paint—as their source of trading signals. They did not understand that the sensory input from the computer was vastly different from the sensory input from the floor. And they continued to try to make decisions from sensory input that no longer existed.

## DISCARDING THE OLD PATTERN

In the rubble of their old patterns and routines were elements that these old floor traders still needed to retain for success as desk traders. Many of these old routines were necessary to signal their brains that they were ready to make money in the markets. For example, they needed to keep getting up at the same time each morning and dressing professionally for work by putting on a trading jacket and tie. These disciplines are harder to follow when you are facing a computer monitor and not a group of your peers. Nevertheless, they are important anchors. And these traders also needed to have the same routine of following the market.

The part of their routine that they were not changing was the decision-making process. They were trying to find opportunity where there was none because the previous rules no longer applied. Would they have the physical stamina, the self-confidence, the capital, the psychological toughness, and the flexibility to discard that old pattern, create a new one, and survive long enough to understand the new set of trading rules? Some did and some did not. What was the difference? The determining factor is the courage to stay flexible, to push the boundaries of those old patterns and to see things in new and unique ways.

## CONCLUSION

Regardless of the changes that a trader may face in the markets or the way in which he trades, he will eventually find himself either avoiding opportunity or being blind to it if he does not continue to stretch his comfort zone. Traders need to be flexible to handle change and see things in new ways in order to correctly perceive opportunity. Instead of shrinking from opportunity because it represents change and discomfort, traders need to continue to take from their old patterns what is useful and discard the rest. They need to build into those patterns the process of ongoing modification and the expansion of experience that allows them to see what works on the ever-changing playing field of the markets. These flexible patterns will allow a trader to continue to feel the good feelings of satisfaction and excitement for the process of trading. These good feelings will not only prevent a trader from sabotaging his trading results in order to feel excitement, they will keep the door to opportunity wide open.

---

*When you give your neurology a pattern of how to focus and repeat it frequently, you will find that focus will then become the path of least resistance.*

---

CHAPTER 30

# Drill to Focus

The ability to focus in the midst of turmoil and emotional stress is an essential in performance excellence for athletes and traders. However, a major obstacle to focus is the infinite distractions that lie in wait like saboteurs. For a world-class gymnast performing in front of a live audience of thousands and a television audience of billions, the distractions tugging at his performance level are no more overwhelming than the distractions surrounding a trader who is making trading decisions that could ultimately bankrupt him.

Like the gymnast, the trader is struggling with the powerful emotions of fear and anticipation that accompany performance. And like the competition floor in gymnastics, the trading arena comes with its own fair share of environmental distractions as well. The trader must contend with phone calls, information overload, family and friends who interrupt, the refrigerator that beckons, and that incessant, loud, nagging inner voice chatter that defines and second guesses every action or decision.

One of the most demanding of all the Olympic competitions is the men's all-around gymnastic event. Paul Hamm, an American gymnast, was leading in the fourth rotation of the competition when he missed his dismount from the vault and nearly plowed into the judges. This mistake dropped him to $12^{th}$ place in the competition. Feeling that he had nothing to lose, he simply focused on his performance on the remaining apparatus and completed the final two events with nearly perfect routines. His effort put him back in first place.

A young American female gymnast named Carly Patterson lost her focus and made a slight mistake in one of her performances in the team competition. The result was a cascade of mistakes as she and her teammates strayed from their course. Instead of earning the gold medal, a rival team, the Romanians, collected the top prize. The difference was the Romanian team, which was evenly matched in sheer talent, never lost focus and made no mistakes.

Days later, Carly Patterson competed again in the individual women's all-around event. As a world-class competitor, she was able to put the mistakes of the previous competition behind her and focus on the challenge at hand. The result was that she was able to win the gold medal from her chief rival, the Russian *prima donna* and world champion, Svetlana Khorkina.

## THE SECRET FORMULA: DRILL

For many years now, I have studied the art of focus and the people who have mastered it in an effort to create a model for others to follow. As a success coach, it became clear to me that the most successful people were the individuals who had learned to focus and were willing to discipline themselves to stay in this exceptional mental state of concentration. As a coach, I have developed a training routine for traders to help them to develop and maintain their focus. To make it easy for traders to remember, I have outlined this training routine into an acronym, DRILL, which perfectly reflects the essence of the exercise. Here is the training drill for developing focus:

- **D—Devour information**. If you want to choose where to aim your focus, you must give yourself a platform of knowledge. Without a solid base of information, the space will fill up with fear and uncertainty.
- **R—Repetition**. You must repeat over and over the actions and strategies that you plan to implement so that it becomes a part of your neurological system and part of your thinking. It has to be in your muscles and the right words have to be in your mind and the passion has to be in your heart. The passion will come from the repetition of the right action.
- **I—Illuminate and ignite with intention.** You must illuminate and ignite the energy centers of your body. You do this with another "I"—Intention. To create this light and energy, focus on the line of energy from the middle of your forehead to the trunk of your body. As you direct your attention to this source of inner energy, you will it (will as in force or determination) to light up as if it were a straight lightning rod.

- **L—Let go.** Once you have created your foundation of knowledge and have ignited your passion through repetition and intention, you must let go. If you try to control the process at this point, your neurological system will begin to change the routine by adding steps that were initially not there. For example, adding a negative step would result in negative emotions.
- **L—Your Last performance does not count.** If you won in your last performance or if you did the best that you possibly could have in your last performance, it does not count, so let it go. If you lost in your last performance, it still does not count. If you try to make up for the previous loss, all you will do is create negative thoughts. The past does not exist. The only thing that counts is this performance, where your focus is now.

This DRILL is a way for traders to remember how to keep on the right path. It is also the same DRILL that Olympic athletes have trained with since they were very young. From the time they enter their chosen sport, these young athletes are immersed in its culture and history. They study the latest techniques and technologies until they have an encyclopedic understanding of everything that is part of and related to their sport. Then, they spend long hours every day repeating the moves that form the basis of their world-class performances so the required moves are etched into their neurology. Finally, in one of the most recent training technologies, they are trained in the art of mental imagery and meditation. This psychological training allows them to harness their mental energies while quieting the mental chatter that tries to distract them.

## THE EASIEST PART OF THE DRILL/THE HARDEST PART OF THE DRILL

The easiest part of the DRILL for most traders is the first part—Devouring the information about trading. Becoming an expert in the markets, reading everything on the shelves, and developing an encyclopedic knowledge of the field involves a great commitment of time and energy. But, for many of the people who go into trading, research and an affinity for technical fields are second nature to them. They feel comfortable seated at a desk or computer reading about challenging mathematical concepts. This is exciting for them. It is also completely risk free. There is a tremendous emotional payoff for this group of traders in the learning phase of the DRILL. Some traders become so comfortable in this phase that they never really move into the hard part of trading, following their system in the face of potential loss.

There are traders who have a tough time with the learning part of the DRILL. For them, the very part that is the easiest for many is the hardest part of all. To make matters worse, a fair proportion of these traders are going into trading for the wrong reason. They crave excitement and think that trading is the pot of gold, the place of easy money to be gained without effort. These traders are essentially gamblers and, with luck, they are washed out very soon.

There are also traders for whom school was never a happy place. Often, they are not technologically oriented. However, some are highly intuitive individuals who have the potential to make great traders if they are willing to tough it out and do the studying that is necessary. If the D part of the DRILL is tough for them, the good news is that the rest of it may turn out to be easy.

Repetition can turn out to be the hardest part for some traders, especially those who have entered the field as potential gamblers. If you are looking for excitement, the act of having to repeat a process over and over again may require far too much patience and delayed gratification for you. For traders who lack inner discipline, practice is strange and hostile territory. But without repetition, a trader is likely to stop following his rules when the pressure is on. It is repetition that causes an Olympic athlete to be able to perform a difficult maneuver when he is competing in front of a TV audience of billions. It is also repetition that can keep a trader from backtracking on his system when his money is on the line.

Some traders are comfortable with repetition. They may have a background in music or sports, where they have long experience in the world of practice, practice, and more practice. They may be highly disciplined, making this the easiest part of the DRILL for them.

The final three parts of the DRILL, igniting and illuminating your energy, letting go of the process, and letting go of the last trade are the hardest parts of the DRILL for traders who have not worked on their psychology. These traders have no experience in the practice of managing their mental and emotional energies. They may also be sabotaged in this effort by unresolved emotional issues from their past that continue to undermine their efforts to succeed. Often, these are the very traders who are the most resistant to working on their psychology. Their own weakness is evident in their fear of appearing to be weak.

For traders who have been working on their psychology and/or have been exploring other tools of personal expansion such as meditation and relaxation techniques, the last three parts of the DRILL may prove to be a walk in the park. Letting go is a technique that is widely practiced in the meditation arts and is also a part of most forms of psychological counseling or therapies. Focusing energy is also a part of many spiritual practices such as yoga and prayer.

## THE SECRET INGREDIENT

Many of the great formulas in life, from great pizza dough to a great marriage, have a secret ingredient. Without the secret ingredient, no amount of recipe duplication will work. Often, people are unaware of the existence of the secret ingredient or they take it for granted. Sometimes, they withhold telling others about the secret ingredient for fear that their success will disappear by sharing the secret.

In the case of the DRILL, there is one secret ingredient that all traders must have for it to work regardless of their past experiences and proclivities. That secret ingredient is commitment. As the old Baltic saying goes, "Nothing changes if nothing changes." But, nothing changes if there is no commitment to change. The DRILL will create the needed momentum for maximum positive change in a trader's life. I have given this DRILL formula to countless traders in one form or another. Some of them have taken it and made it work so well for them that they are now some of the most successful traders in the field. I have also given it to traders who have failed to live up to their potential.

- They see all of the reasons that it cannot work for them.
- They find ways to sabotage their efforts.
- They complain and make excuses.
- They only implement the parts of the DRILL that are easy for them.
- They practice the DRILL with half their heart.
- They practice the DRILL half the time.

What is missing for these lackluster traders is their commitment to success. Unfortunately, no one can give you a magical formula for being committed. Commitment comes from deep within a person. Once again, the Olympic athletes who took our breath away as they performed miraculous feats of strength and agility all shared that same secret ingredient. They could never reach their level of performance without making a total commitment to their sport and to winning.

If you want to commit to practicing the DRILL but are questioning your level of commitment, you might ask yourself the following questions:

- Am I willing to follow a discipline every day without fail?
- How disciplined am I?

- What has been my history of following a discipline?
- How much do I want to succeed as a trader? What am I willing to do? What would I be willing to give up?
- Have I already formed an escape plan in case of failure?
- Am I planning for failure? Am I afraid of success?

The honest answers to these questions will give you a good idea of how committed you are and what kind of success you will have in following the DRILL. If you can see that your level of commitment is low, you may want to do some serious soul-searching about your real goals in life. If you discover that your level of commitment is high, then DRILL away!

## CONCLUSION

For traders who want to succeed, there is much to be learned about focus from Olympic athletes. Focus allows them to keep their eyes on the prize through the conclusion of the competition. The great 35-year-old Brazilian distance runner, Vanderlei de Lima, was on his way to winning the gold medal in the marathon when a violent onlooker tackled him and dragged him into the crowd. De Lima managed to escape his attacker and regain his focus. Somehow, he got himself back into the race and finished third to earn the bronze medal. Sticking to a DRILL is what makes it possible for world-class athletes and traders to stay focused in the face of extreme distractions. Our DRILL provides a commitment to building a foundation of knowledge, consistent repetition, the direction of energy, and the practice of letting go of the future outcome and everything that has happened in the past.

PART V

# Modeling Top Traders

*The heart is the bridge that leads to a state of the extraordinary.*

CHAPTER 31

# The Heart of a Master Trader

Over the years, many people have asked if becoming a Master Trader is something that you can develop. Just like in any field where mastery is sought, there are those exceptional individuals who seem to be born with it or to have had the good fortune to be born into it. However, one important characteristic that makes someone who achieves greatness stand out is heart.

So what is this thing called heart? It is:

- Having enough burning desire to break through all personal limitations
- Having the sensitivity to know how to balance breaking through your limitations without physically and emotionally breaking down
- Having enough courage to stand up to all the people who are against you
- Taking the kind of calculated risks that few would dare to take
- Going against others when they say the task is impossible
- Being willing to sacrifice almost anything to achieve the desired goal
- Being willing to conquer yourself
- Recognizing that strengths must be improved upon and weaknesses must be compensated for or overcome and turned into greater strengths
- Not allowing excuses, good reasons, or logical explanations to keep you from your goals

Then the question that should be asked is: "Can you develop the heart of a trader, or is it some mysterious gift that is given to a lucky few?"

Circumstances, experience, skill, and talent do make a difference in having heart. Most skills and talents can be developed and some circumstances and experiences can be created. But heart comes from a combination of these things and then goes a good distance beyond that.

Let's explore three situations that create the environment that seeds the heart of a master.

## "BA-DA-BING"

It is certainly easier to become a baseball star when your father was Cal Ripken, Sr. Cal Sr.'s passion for teaching the craft of baseball ran deep and his knowledge was passed on to his son Cal Ripken, Jr., who became a Baseball Hall of Famer by redefining the position of shortstop.

Cal Ripken, Jr. is known as baseball's all-time Iron Man. He was one of only seven players in the history of the game to amass 400 home runs and 3,000 hits in his career. In 1995, Ripken broke Lou Gehrig's record for consecutive games played. Ripkin's mark of 2,632 consecutive games played is likely to endure for generations to come.

How about the Forbes' family dynasty? It is certainly easier to become a master of publishing when your father was Malcolm Forbes.

There are many people on the financial speaking circuit who purport humbly to be master traders. They might have had a time of glory, but now they are only as good as their advertising. Then, there are those traders like Chuck, known by only a few other people for their top skills as traders and who like it that way. Chuck's father and uncle were both highly skilled speculators and they fed Chuck with the golden spoon of trading mastery. While Chuck heard many horror stories about traders failing in the markets, his focus was on how easy it was to earn a good living as a trader simply by following his uncle's and his dad's lead. Chuck became even more successful than his family and was respected for being generous with both his knowledge and his time.

There are many families who offer nurturing environments and have the means and desire to support their children to become masters at anything they want to pursue. However, this does not guarantee exceptional success. The spark of relentless desire has to be ignited from within the individual to achieve this top performance. And even this spark is no guarantee for greatness. Like the song says in the musical *Damn Yankees*, "Ya Gotta Have Heart."

## THE MINE FIELD

The second set of circumstances that create an environment for heart and mastery comes from those who overcome tremendous adversity. Having what it takes to conquer exceptionally difficult circumstances gives you the endurance to conquer yourself and become a master.

### Enter Sea Biscuit

I saw the movie *Sea Biscuit*, which is a true story about how several people and one horse combined their efforts to create a champion. To make this happen, they had to be in the right place at the right time, experience wonderful triumphs, face great difficulties, and make unusually risky choices. All of them faced great adversity and each of them developed the heart of a winner.

They also had the unique gift of being able to recognize the heart in each other. The horse's owner lost his son in an accident that he blamed himself for. He also lost his wife because she blamed him, too. He needed an opportunity to overcome his sadness and guilt. The trainer, who was living from hand to mouth, needed someone to recognize his special talent for connecting with animals. He was presented with an opportunity to train a horse of his choice.

As a teen, the jockey had to leave his family because they could no longer afford to support him. He longed for the opportunity to prove that he was the special person that his father wanted him to be. Of course, there was Sea Biscuit. He needed an environment of nurturing to show his breeding, talent, and ability to be a winner. Sea Biscuit was the ultimate result of what heart can do for the soul of man. His triumph brought a nation together after the bitter days of the the Great Depression by giving people hope for the future.

There are many people throughout history who have overcome great odds and adversity in their quest for greatness. Here are some people with heart.

- Dr. Milton Erickson, who in spite of polio, became the greatest hypnotherapist of all time
- Tiger Woods, who in spite of the race barrier, became one of the greatest golfers of all time
- Lance Armstrong, who in spite of cancer in his lungs and brain, won the Tour de France five times in a row

- Thomas Edison, who was sent home from school because the teachers said he was too stupid to learn anything, became one of the greatest inventors in history
- Benjamin Franklin was the fifteenth of seventeen children of a poor candle maker. His first obstacle was that he had only one year of schooling. He went on to teach himself philosophy, four languages, the classics, writing for publication, science, finance, politics, diplomacy, becoming one of the best educated and greatest Americans.
- Annette Kellerman was a sickly and lame woman who became the World Diving Champion and was judged the world's most perfectly formed woman.

In the rags to riches stories that I have collected over the years, there are a few that I think about when I go through a challenging time in my own life. One that stands out to me is a trader named Roger. He was born into a family that had a difficult time keeping food on the table and a roof over their heads. His father was in a wheelchair and took care of the three children at home. His mother, who had very little education, worked on a candy factory production line. Roger did what he could as the oldest son to help support the family by becoming a paperboy and doing other odd jobs. Since he was unable to finish high school, he thought that he was destined to do blue collar work for the rest of his days. Until the day that changed his life.

Roger was in the habit of doing good deeds for people because he saw his father and mother help others despite their difficulties. He learned from a very young age that good deeds gave you good feelings. With all of the sad moments in his life, he longed for good feelings. So, he looked for opportunities to help others.

Roger was working as a maintenance man in an office building in Chicago. One day, he found in the restroom a briefcase filled with important and valuable items such as contracts and certificates. An executive at the Chicago Board Options Exchange had accidentally left it there. Roger returned it intact and the man wanted to reward him for his honesty. The man was impressed with Roger and asked about his life. He wanted to know how a good-looking, honorable young man was cleaning buildings for a living.

After Roger told him about his life, the man offered him a job as a runner at the CBOE. Runner led to trader, trader led to super trader, and super trader was able to send his brothers and sister to school and give his parents a more comfortable life.

While Roger seemed to have been given his break when he became a runner, his training for becoming a trader started from overcoming his difficult life and recognizing the value of good deeds.

## TRUE GRIT

Yes, there is opportunity for creating heart beyond adversity and being born into it. This third set of circumstances are for those who:

- Set their sights on a goal for mastery with tasks that are developed out of a good plan
- Seek out good models and mentors
- Develop the discipline necessary to follow good rules consistently
- Create a nurturing supportive environment
- Become a constant student of the markets
- Balance all areas of life to support mastery
- Handle psychological issues that create sabotage
- Work with a success coach
- Become a mentor to others

Suzy was a woman who sought out what she wanted and did whatever it took to be the best she could be. She was a high achiever in school and in the corporate world. Then, she became a top multi-level marketing consultant while creating a nurturing home for her family. Suzy's husband was looking for a new career after retirement and in the process, he and Suzy both became interested in trading. She transferred the experience of her multi-marketing skills into becoming successful as a trader. Working side by side with her husband and using the same formula for success, Suzy blossomed into becoming a master trader while her husband developed into a good trader.

The fact is that with the right formula those with the heart of a trader will blossom and others will only be good. But in trading, "good ain't bad."

## STRAY BULLET OF GREATNESS

There is another form of greatness that I need to mention. There are those people, who in the process of seeking out one form of success, achieve it in another way.

One of the most talented people that I know in the financial field has written several best-selling financial books. He is an exceptional trading teacher and has developed several profitable trading systems. He is one of the best in the world at analyzing markets. The only problem is that his target was to become a great trader and this success has eluded him. He has solved his problem by having someone else pull the trigger on trades for him. While he has experienced the rewards of greatness, there is a part of him that would give it all up to become a great trader.

## CONCLUSION

I believe that the heart of a trader can be developed. Yes, it is easier for some because of their experiences and resources, but even the best of traders may not reach their top performance if they do not follow a good model. The fortunate thing about working on becoming a great trader is that there is always more than one winner. Even if you only become a good trader, in trading "good ain't bad."

---

*If you think like a trader and act like a trader you will not think you are a duck.*

---

CHAPTER 32

# Top Performance

Are you willing to do what is necessary to become a top performance trader? Before you answer "Yes" to this question, I want to fill you in as to what this response entails.

Consider this list the price that must be paid to achieve the rewards that come from top trading performance:

Education
Time
Money
Energy
Sacrifice
Conquering Yourself
Risk

Unfortunately, the price is too high for most people and they stop short of completing the actions that are necessary. We all like to think of ourselves as above average, but most of us only manage to be exceptional at coming up with good excuses for maintaining a level of mediocrity.

Most professions require at least a college or graduate degree as a minimum barrier of entry. While there are a few universities that grant degrees with a concentration in trading, most traders must educate themselves on the job. It is an exceptionally difficult assignment to constantly motivate yourself to overcome each new task on the way to becoming a good trader. This says nothing about becoming a top performance trader when most want-to-be traders meet with discouragement and move on to something new.

If you are one of those starry-eyed want-to-be traders or an average trader who has determined to become a top performance trader, read on and take the actions that those who have reached high levels of performance have taken.

## EDUCATION

To be a top performer in trading, you must have a basic foundation of knowledge of the markets and a thorough understanding of trading techniques and methodology. Beyond that, you need an education in the psychology of the markets and must have the discipline necessary to stick to your business plan and your criteria for entering and exiting trades. The more education you have in trading, the more prepared you will be to adapt to the inevitable changes that occur in the markets and stay the course for a long trading career.

Over the years, I have found that a trader will be more likely to add the intuitive/discretionary indicator that is necessary to become a master trader if he has more education.

## TIME

Most of us have lives with little time to spare. When trying to add a new activity to our busy schedules, we find that it creates a major stress factor. I am certain that each of you has convincing arguments to justify the necessity of activities to maintain your life. Nevertheless, the fact remains that without a change in time priorities, trading success will remain beyond your reach.

If you want to re-prioritize your time, a good first step would be to develop a time chart that lists all of the activities needed for a balanced life. Next, prioritize the remaining activities.

Now, put trading on top of the entire list. If your basic needs consume all of your time or if other activities take priority over trading, then do not bother considering trading. Remember, your life must be in balance if it is to support your trading. Even though your initial enthusiasm for the business of trading may prompt you to replace all of your other activities, you will eventually sabotage your efforts if your life is not balanced.

## MONEY

It takes money to make money. Initially, you need money to lay the foundation for your trading business. This initial need comes in the form of money for education, for research, and for development of a methodology. Then, you need money to maintain and operate your trading business. Finally, you need money for inventory to allow you to take the risks that are necessary to earn more money. The more money you have, the less you should have to risk.

Overall, most businesses fail because they are undercapitalized. Too many traders go into the business of trading undercapitalized because they fail to follow the universal business rules regarding adequate capitalization. A wise strategy is to salt away trading capital while educating yourself. This strategy will give you a running start when you are ready to trade.

## ENERGY

Your life choices determine how much energy you have on any given day. Success is more likely to follow if you are able to focus more concentrated energy on your trading when you first start. After you are initially successful, you can decrease the time you spend trading. Nevertheless, it is important to maintain focused energy when you are making trading decisions.

If you want to increase your ability to maintain that concentrated, focused energy for trading, you should commit to decreasing the energy sappers mentioned in Chapter 6. A quick cheat-sheet is as follows:

- Make healthy eating choices
- Drink plenty of water
- Keep away from substances like coffee and alcohol
- Sleep at least seven hours at night
- Exercise every day
- Resolve the conflicts in your life
- Heal emotional issues
- Monitor your energy level when making trading choices
- Ask yourself if you are in a peak performance state when you are trading—physically, emotionally, and mentally, and if you are not, quit for the day

## SACRIFICE

It is important to balance the activities in your life to keep from sabotaging your trading results. Achieving the balance that allows you to concentrate time and energy to reach your goals will require that you sacrifice some of your activities. To achieve your goals, you need to gain the cooperation and support of your family and friends. Ask them to provide you with the encouragement that you need to achieve these goals. Make sure the people in your life understand that holidays and other special occasions that take time away from your trading day may initially have to be sacrificed to reach your goals. It is important that everyone understands this reality because it prevents you from feeling guilty when you have to say "No" at some time.

Ask people in your life if they will sign an agreement to provide the kind of support that you need to become a trader. Later, when they are trying to be time-grabbers, you can remind them of their signed agreement and let them know how you appreciate their consideration in helping you reach your goals.

## CONQUERING YOURSELF

Trading is a trip of self-discovery and a profession that can earn you a great deal of money in the process. The former becomes more important to traders after they earn a comfortable living. The more work you do to conquer your psychological issues, the easier it will be to attain and maintain peak performance.

Those traders that are pro-active in handling the issues that keep them from following their trading rules will be less likely to start trading with large losses. Most people who enter the trading business do not know this. It comes as a total surprise to them to discover that they need help with trading psychology to succeed. Many traders lose a lot of money before discovering that they need help. A good question to ask along the way is, "Would I make more money if I were more consistent in following my rules?"

## TRUSTING TO RISK

You will never achieve great levels of success without taking risk. To be highly successful as a trader, you must trust your business plan, your trading method, and yourself to take the calculated risks that are necessary to achieve success. When new traders face the possibility of loss, they tend to concentrate their energy on each loss rather than the big picture of earning money. It is difficult for most people to trust their system, even one that is well tested, when their hard-earned money is being swept away by the markets.

If you do not trust your system, you will continue to experience conflict in decision making after the first few losses. For that reason, it is essential to back or forward test your system before you start to trade real money.

If you cannot trust yourself to make trading decisions at the right time or if you break the trading rules of your system, then consider the following:

- Do not trade
- Find someone to coach you
- Have someone else make the trades

## CONCLUSION

The profession of trading is not for everyone. You need to have the motivation and commitment to work on your own with a scarcity of support that would be atypical if you were working in another profession. You must also make the sacrifices of time and energy that are necessary for success. As in any business, you need the financial resources to support the business, yourself, and the risk required to create wealth. Trading is a profession where you must conquer your own psychological demons to find the discipline necessary to be successful. Even though this price is very steep, if it sounds like one that you are willing to pay, then trading is right for you.

---

*The rite of passage for a trader is to overcome the fear of past experiences.*

---

CHAPTER 33

# The Rite of Passage for a Professional Trader

The journey to becoming a successful professional is a trader's Rite of Passage. Just as a child must experience many challenges on his way to adulthood, a trader must face and overcome a set of hurdles. Each step in the rite of passage brings the trader to the next step in becoming a true professional.

## THE FIRST STEP IS THE HARDEST

Richard was anxious to trade. He had toyed with the notion of trading for a year after taking early retirement from his career as a computer systems developer. After reading several books about the markets, attending a seminar on trading, and putting together his first trading system, he determined that he was ready to start. The problem was that Richard wanted to run before he had taken his first step. With the same enthusiasm that he had applied to his first career, he began trading his system in real time with his accumulated trading capital. Unfortunately, he had not fully tested his system, which he justified as an unnecessary expenditure of time and effort since he had already done his reading and research. Richard had not completed this rite of passage and failed as a trader. He washed out of trading as his system failed him and he failed his system.

## THE RITES OF PASSAGE

Just as Richard failed one of the early rites of passage for a professional trader, many others fail to achieve their professional goals because they either fail to complete one of the required steps or they do not recognize the need to complete a step at all.

What is a rite of passage? All cultures establish significant events or ceremonies marking the transition from one stage of life to another. One of the most meaningful events in more primitive cultures is the rite of passage into manhood for 12- or 13-year-old male children. In this rite, a man-child leaves the tribe to survive in the wilderness for a time while achieving some sign of physical prowess and bravery such as hunting and killing a wild animal. Thus, a rite of passage is that test of commitment and courage associated with reaching the next stage of success, development, and social acceptance.

In the modern world, we are surrounded by unofficially recognized rites of passage including graduation, the first job, buying the first car, buying the first home, getting married, having the first child, putting your children through college, retirement, and so on. Each culture and profession has its own rites of passage. Trading has established an unwritten series of rites of passage for an individual to reach the pinnacle of being a successful professional trader.

The rites of passage for a professional trader are as follows.

### Raising the Capital Required to Begin Trading

There is little doubt that raising the capital necessary to begin trading is one of the greatest single challenges that face an aspiring trader. I have worked with traders who have saved money for decades before amassing sufficient capital to begin trading. Having succeeded at this difficult test, these traders are positioned to succeed exceptionally or fail just as wildly. It is important to understand that the achievement of one rite constitutes no guarantee of success. It merely permits entry into the next stage.

It is important to understand what it means to raise the needed capital to trade. This step is crucial to future success. Insufficient trading capital is the single most common reason that new traders fail. As a trader learns his profession, mistakes can take the form of losses. An airplane that is in trouble can still land if given a long enough runway, but without a sufficient runway, that same airplane will crash and burn. The same principle applies to a trader. This rite of passage does not apply to all traders because of family wealth or employment where inventory for trading is supplied by an institution. It is imperative that a trader does not grant himself a pass on this rite of passage before its requirements have been satisfied fully.

### Completing the Research

When a trader has passed this test, it is a very empowering. At this point, a trader feels confident that he has read what must be read, researched the markets that must be understood, and educated himself before working on his trading system. At this point, he understands the markets and trading but realizes that this information is still theoretical. If his research has been done properly, the trader is prepared to withstand public scrutiny, just like a young Jewish boy who is asked to answer questions directed at him by the rabbi in front of his family and synagogue during his Bar Mitzvah.

This rite of passage does confer the right to begin designing a trading system. Unfortunately, many eager new traders are unwilling to complete the requirements of this rite of passage. Rather than investing the long months and years to complete this preparation, these traders take the easy road, which is also the fastest way to the exit.

### Developing the System

Justin did not develop his own system. He bought a carefully tested system designed by a brilliant and successful trader. There would have been nothing wrong with sidestepping this particular rite of passage if he had done his research and preparation. However, he was ill equipped to understand what was happening with his system because he had failed to do his reading. He did not understand the fact that all systems contain built-in losses nor did he understand what was triggering those losses. As a result, he stopped trusting his system and began to second-guess it. The result was that he washed out of trading early and demanded his money back for the system he purchased.

For the trader who spends the time to create his own system, the result is a love affair that defies description. The first system is a thing of beauty and a symbol of a major achievement. It is also the ticket to the game, except not as a player—not yet.

### Fully Testing Your System

For many traders, a fully tested system is the most significant rite of passage. Putting together a system and testing it can be a long-term assignment for a detail-oriented/risk-averse trader. Real-time paper trading, historical trading, and system testing services offer important views of a system's viability in various markets and timeframes. Once a system has been exhaustively tested, a trader learns what his system can do, its expected profit-to-loss ratio, and how to work with its signals and he officially becomes a trader. It is the equivalent of a college degree and he is no longer just an observer of the markets. He is now a player. Without a fully tested system, a trader is a gambler or an amateur.

### Completing a Detailed Business Plan

A professional trader is also a businessman. He works for himself, manages money, raises money, manages an office, and directly and/or indirectly employs a small number of individuals. If a trader wants to stay in business, he must operate by the principles of business management, which includes having a business plan. This plan provides a detailed model of the trading operation, an inventory of assets and liabilities, a list of resources, projected costs and income, and a plan for the future including contingencies.

It should take a few months to complete a comprehensive business plan because it requires research, data collection, contemplation, and the answers to some very tough questions. The most important people to a business, including bankers and clients, expect such a business plan and that it be professional, complete and transparent. A trader may begin trading before completing the business plan, but he is not officially in business until it is completed. Thus, a business plan, complete and comprehensive, is another rite of passage.

### Working on Your Psychology

Successful professional traders know that their greatest enemy is in their own minds. The emotions of fear and greed are more powerful than any market forces in creating losses. Unresolved issues from a trader's past can show up when a trader is bored, frightened, worried, or thinking about anything that could remind his unconscious of forgotten events.

The psychology of trading is recognized as a major issue in maintaining a trading career. For this reason, traders who are committed to long-term careers are lining up to deal with their psychological and emotional issues and working on their self-discipline. This type of work is just as demanding as the research and development phase of a trader's career. Having completed this work is like being handed the key to the kingdom, giving you freedom to trade at your optimum level.

### Surviving the First Major Loss

The pain and fear that accompanies a major loss is often sufficient to put a trader out of business. Too often, a trader is ill prepared for the disorientation that results from a single large loss or string of losses. He can read and talk about it, but there is no way to adequately prepare for it until it happens. However, if the trader is supported by a pool of trading capital that is large enough to absorb the loss(es) and his emotional pool is deep enough to absorb the shock waves, a trader can deal with the loss and regain his forward momentum.

Regardless of talent or system profitability, a trader will sustain losses. How well the losses are handled largely determines how long a trader can trade afterward. Preparing to handle loss is part of the rite of passage. If a trader trusts his system, amasses adequate trading capital, works on his psychology, follows his business plan, considers contingencies in his business plan, and puts into place the personal supports necessary to sustain him through losses, he will survive this major challenge.

The first major win can be as traumatic as the first major loss. The emotional roller coaster ride that accompanies the first major win can be as unsettling to stability and self-discipline as the first major loss. For this reason, the same supports need to be put into place to survive this trial, as well.

### Surviving the First Major Market Change

No trading system can predict every potential move or work in every market. Flexibility must be factored into every trader's system. Even the most flexible trader cannot predict the type of random market changes that occur. Countless traders were hit broadside when their exchanges converted to electronic trading formats.

In a long trading career, a trader should expect to endure at least one major market change that turns his trading system and style on its head. When markets undergo these profound changes, the unprepared traders wash out. Once again, the trader who has worked on his psychology has an advantage in adversity because he has the emotional resources to handle it. If he has built a strong family and social net to sustain him and has managed his finances and risk carefully, he will have the ability to weather a dramatic change in the markets because market change has been considered in his contingency planning.

### Developing an Intuitive Trading Signal

Once the technical aspects and psychological issues of trading have been addressed, a trader may want to explore the next realm of trading by using an intuitive signal. This step is truly a rite of passage because it requires such a long stage of preparation before a trader is tuned into his trading, his system, and the markets that he can recognize and trust his intuitive signals. Too often, rookie traders attempt this last great rite because they fail to see how much preparation and experience are required. For inexperienced traders to attempt this strategy is like a new skater trying to perform stationary spins because they look so easy. Most techniques used by masters look deceptively simple until one tries to duplicate them. From observation, the profits generated by intuitive master traders are by far the most significant ones in the industry. This rite of passage gives a trader a rightful step onto the top of the trading pyramid and represents a significant body of preparation and hard-won experience.

## CONCLUSION

Like all professions, trading presents its members with a set of great challenges that lead to higher steps in development and success. Each rite of passage represents a trader's commitment to excellence and growth and requires qualities of character such as courage, determination, and persistence. With each rite of passage, a trader moves closer to becoming a successful professional trader at the top of his form. For this reason, it is important to recognize these rites and to celebrate them for what they represent and for where they are leading.

---

*Whatever the success model you follow, you still need to fit yourself into that model and sometimes the fit will need major alterations in order to grow.*

---

CHAPTER 34

# Middle C

A struggling young client asked me recently: "At what point will I be a real trader?"

I told him. "You become a trader, a real trader, once you visualize in your mind that you are a trader and have a very clear picture of being a trader. At that moment, regardless of your education, knowledge, or experience, you are a trader."

He looked at me doubtfully when I had given my reply. So, I continued. "The only things that will separate you from that picture are the other pictures created in your mind that make you question yourself."

When you imagine yourself as a trader, you cloak yourself in the suit of a trader. You start eating, walking, and doing the things that traders do because your decision to be a trader will attract all that is necessary for you to become a trader.

If you doubt the power of your own mental imagery, close your eyes for a moment. Clearly visualize that you are confronting a possible trade, but do not know what to do. You feel powerless to pull the trigger. You feel frightened and in the dark about everything that is happening around you. Filled with self-doubt and a lack of confidence, how do you think you will face the next trade when your eyes are wide open?

## VIRTUOSO IN MIDDLE C

Recently, I attended a party at which the host announced that his children wanted to entertain me on the piano.

The first child to perform was the eldest girl of the family. She sat down at the keyboard with a tremendous amount of confidence, which prompted me to expect that I was about to hear something quite extraordinary. When she began to play, my expectations were immediately realized. Upon concluding her sterling performance, she closed with a simple bow. We applauded her performance enthusiastically because it was truly amazing. After her bow, she identified the title of the piece that she had just played.

The next child to perform was her younger brother. Prior to playing, he approached the bench with equal confidence. Modeling his older sister, the boy settled himself confidently on the seat. While his performance showed that he had a ways to go before he would match his sister's artistic mastery, the simplicity of his performance was equally entertaining. I could see from his parents' reactions that their son had played the best that he could at his present level of mastery. For that, they were equally supportive and pleased. After his performance, the younger brother also bowed and announced the title of his piece.

The third child to entertain us was another girl, who was only four years old. She approached the bench with the same confidence as her older brother and sister. She paused before her performance and with focus that was equal to her older siblings, raised the pointer finger on her right hand and pressed the key of Middle C. Then, she stood up, bowed with a flourish and announced, "The name of my piece is 'Middle C.'" We all applauded her enthusiastically because she had also done the best she could. The best for her was the knowledge that the picture she had in her mind would manifest itself in time.

## MAKE IT SO, NUMBER ONE!

The pictures that you create in your mind are really instructions to your unconscious mind. The general instruction from each and every mental image is identical, even if the actual images are completely different. The general instruction from these mental images is the same as the command given by Captain Jean Luc Picard of the starship Enterprise to his First Officer. When Captain Picard issued a command, it was always accompanied by the phrase, "Make it so, Number One!"

In the case of your own mind dramas, your mental picture is the Commander and your unconscious mind is its First Officer, condemned to carry out its every order without question. To your unconscious mind, your picture of reality *is* the reality. It must do whatever is needed to "make it so." Two facts about these mental pictures give them power to structure your reality:

1. They are directives that must be obeyed
2. Since they are operating on an unconscious level, they are very difficult to identify and even more difficult to influence

## FUZZY PICTURES AND BAD RECEPTION

To be effective, your mental picture must be positive and it must be in clear focus. I once worked with a trader named Dave, who was having great difficulty pulling his trading together. His responses to questions about his professional and personal life were invariably vague. If his responses to my questions were murky, his mental pictures were even more indistinct. Despite his expressed desire to be a highly successful trader, he simply could not picture himself filling the role of a successful trader. In fact, Dave could not clearly picture himself as a trader at all.

However, he could clearly picture himself as the manager of a successful restaurant, which was the career that he had abandoned in favor of trading. He had convinced himself that trading was a lucrative field and that he could make a great deal of money in it. When he discussed his trading business, he had no passion for it. But, Dave lit up like a 1000-watt bulb when he discussed his experiences in the world of restaurant management.

He showed me pictures of his old restaurants and of the people that he had trained. In his mind's eye, he was running a busy restaurant, training staff, catering to his clientele, and enjoying the satisfaction derived from providing great service to the public. It did not require a great deal of work to convince him to surrender his trading dream in favor of the world his imagination had already perceived as his reality.

How do you know if your mental picture is a fuzzy one? The more detail a picture has, the more in-focus it will become. For example, can you answer these questions when you picture yourself trading?

- Where are you?
- What does the room look like?
- What sounds can you hear? Is the room silent or is there music playing? If so, what song is playing?
- Exactly what are you doing?
- What kind of trading are you doing?
- What system are you using to make your decisions?
- How big are the trades that you are making?
- What is the market doing?
- What are you wearing?
- How much money is in your trading account?

- How do you feel? What is your emotional state? Are you happy, frightened, upset, joyful, or expectant?
- How successful do you think you are at this moment?
- What picture is in your mind of your future? Describe it.

If you can answer these questions clearly, then you are a real trader. If you cannot answer them or if your answers lack detail, you are giving yourself fuzzy mental pictures of yourself as a trader. The result is that you are swimming against the tide.

If a television station broadcasts fuzzy images, you can expect poor reception on your home screen. No matter how much you fuss with your television or complain to your cable operator, the images will continue to be unreadable. The problem with fuzzy mental images is that you are transmitting fuzzy instructions to your unconscious. Your unconscious mind will not know what to do and may do all of the wrong things or do nothing at all. In the case of some fuzzy images that are a jumble of positive and negative pictures, you might be sabotaging yourself each time you take a step forward.

## SENDING CLEAR MENTAL PICTURES

Like the four-year-old pianist who played Middle C with maestro self-possession, you can lay the groundwork for success as a trader by building the clearest and most powerful mental image of success. If your desire to be a successful trader is stronger than any other dream but you do not have the mental image, you can create a mental picture that will guide your unconscious to act the role and "make it so."

One of the most effective ways to create a new mental image is to sit down with a pad of paper and construct a detailed profile of a successful trader. The optimum way to do this is to have a prototype or best-possible example to model. From reading about trading masters, you can extract details, attitudes, and behaviors that can be used. From your own experiences and observations, you can add attitudes and behaviors that also resulted in success.

Put it all down on paper. Write a description of yourself as a great, successful trader and do not omit any details: Describe the place, the sounds, the smells, the office arrangement, and what you are wearing. Describe precisely what you are doing, how you are feeling, and what you are saying to yourself as you are doing it. The description of the mental image should be so clear that a movie director, set designer, and actor could recreate the scene exactly.

Once you have the picture, read it over and over until you know each detail to the point that you can close your eyes and see, hear, smell, and feel it. The picture should include a scene where you are watching a signal from your system, taking that signal, watching the trade as it zigzags in the appropriate direction, and then successfully exiting the trade. As you exit that successful trade, your mental picture should include an image of you celebrating your success and repeating the cycle over and over.

## CONCLUSION

A detailed mental image is one of the most powerful tools that a trader can have. An individual with a clear vision of himself as a trader, with positive detail and without misgiving, is truly a trader. Once we can clearly see the vision of ourselves doing or being a particular thing, the experience of it exists for us. When the clear picture is created in our minds, the image of reality becomes real for us and we send instructions to our unconscious mind that must be followed to make it so. At this point, we set into motion the forces that will do whatever it takes to make that image become a reality. In fact, the reality of that vision is already manifested in the future. We may not be able to play Tchaikovsky's *Piano Concerto No. 1* yet, but if we can see ourselves doing it, we are well on the way to reaching our goals.

---

*Passion is the fuel to an unstoppable path.*

---

CHAPTER 35

# Passion

The secret to great trading is to have the passion that builds motivation. Passion supports the discipline that is necessary in overcoming the psychological pain of draw-downs and the turmoil of market reversals, and focuses you on a path to making real money.

## CREATING PASSION

How do you create passion in yourself, and is it possible to create passion where there was little or none before? This question is one often asked by traders who have lost their passion for trading. The answer is a qualified yes.

First, let us look at the state of your passion right now. Answer the following eight questions with a score from one to five, with five being the most positive answer:

1. You would do the work even if you did not get paid for it
2. You are focused on mastery in your trading
3. You notice a transformation of yourself, not just the outcome of work
4. You are unaware of time passing when you are trading
5. You find that you become creative as well as technical in your approach to trading

6. You avoid short cuts and expediencies in achieving your goals in trading
7. You require very little rest and awaken eager to get started
8. You spend little to no time thinking about vacations from trading

Any responses to these issues in the one-to-two range show a low level of passion for your trading. You should find your answers in the four-to-five range for all the questions if you are to have a level of passion that can bring you to a high level of success.

To understand how you can increase your level of passion, it is important to understand where passion comes from and how, if at all, you can mine these sources for your own use.

## THE GREAT LACKING

Some of the most passionate traders I have worked with came from very difficult circumstances. They were raised in great poverty or they escaped war-torn countries or they were forced, for whatever reasons, to do without the things that those around them had, thereby making them feel powerless, vulnerable, and angry at the injustice of their poverty. All of this great lacking creates in some children the insatiable need to achieve so that they will never again feel the pain of not having what they need. This great ambition to achieve is what drove men like Andrew Carnegie to build financial empires and to never be satisfied with what they had. There is a great passion in this unconscious need to overcome these early feelings of helplessness, want, and vulnerability by creating enormous wealth. The resulting drive for success is so unstoppable that the elements of a balanced and happy personal life are often ignored or rejected, especially if they are seen to interfere with the end goal of success.

Fred was one of these traders. He was so passionate about his trading that he worked 15 hours a day, six and seven days a week at his trading. Fred was undeterred by losses, market reversals, and system problems. He was eager to learn everything he could about trading and was even willing to work on his trading psychology as long as it was finely honed in on his trading. Although Fred's family was not poor, his father had come through the Great Depression of the 1930s with such a fear of poverty that he had kept his wife and children on a deprivation diet of parsimony, as he squirreled away every penny he could save for the rainy day that he knew was coming. The result for Fred was a childhood of going to bed on an empty stomach and going to school in hand-me-down clothes. Fred made a decision that he would never go hungry again.

If you are motivated by fear, the best way to mine this source is to increase your level of fear of failure and vividly imagine what it would be like to lose everything. This picture is enough to get some people very passionate about their trading. For others, it could have the opposite affect.

Although this is possibly the most powerful source of passion for success in trading, it is one source that some of you may not want to create. You need to know yourself. Are you motivated by seeing yourself with a very negative outcome or by seeing positive images of what you could become in the future?

## THE LOVE OF THE THING

Some children are just born with a passion for a particular thing, whether it is baseball or cars or horses or playing the piano. And no adult can talk them out of it. These passions seem to be hard-wired and are probably the result of genetics at its best. These individuals find the source of their passion and pursue it despite all obstacles in their path. An innate love of numbers and finance or a love of the roar and excitement of the trading floor has driven more than one passionate trader into the profession. And no amount of setbacks can deter these traders.

This kind of passion cannot be manufactured by argument, logic, counseling, or a change in circumstance. It can only be unearthed. Sometimes, an individual with this kind of passion is unable to access it because he has not yet encountered the trigger to release it. For example, a child has an innate passion for racing, but does not see a race until he is in his young adulthood. Once he sees his first race, his life is transformed and there is no going back.

Sometimes, this passion is crushed or purposely squeezed out of a child because the people around him are either threatened by this passion or they do not understand it. When this occurs, the individual spends his life feeling an emptiness that he cannot explain, and he wonders why he feels no passion for the things that he has chosen to do. I have counseled many such individuals.

Do all of us have an innate love of the thing? I believe that most of us do. Our job is to discover what that thing is and overcome our fear of pursuing it in a way that is fulfilling to us. One of the successful ways to use this motivating source for trading is to look at the various elements of trading.

Do you have a deep love of one or more of these elements, and if so, which one? Naturally, the more elements you enjoy, the more likely trading is the profession for you. Think about your love for the following:

- **Research and Analysis**—those who are attracted to analytical study, as a result of their backgrounds in engineering and mathematics, will find this part of the trading process extremely enjoyable. Very often these are the same people who find it difficult to deal with the emotions of trading when they actually have to put on a trade because this is stretching into an area that is unfamiliar to them.
- **Risk and Competition**—those who enjoy athletics, war games, and computer games will find this part of trading stimulating and exciting. This stimulation will keep a trader coming back each day with a sense of anticipation like a hunter going out seeking his prey. However, once a trader has been in the profession for a number of months, he might find that following a system is like watching wet paint dry and the original thrill of the hunt could be gone, which can lead to some psychological challenges.
- **Conquering Yourself**—initially, when a trader comes into trading it is all about making money, but eventually, he finds out it is all about conquering himself because to stay in the markets and be successful he must conquer all of his fears and demons. This process then becomes his new challenge and those who enjoy this process are on their way to mastery.

## BIOLOGY IS DESTINY

Scientists have discovered the biological basis for what we normally call passion is in our neurotransmitters, the chemicals that ebb and flow in the synapses of our brains. Such neurochemicals as dopamine and beta-endorphins can make us feel a great urge to satisfy our appetites. In addition, our hormones also feed into our passions. A while back, NPR produced a program that examined the relationship between testosterone and personality. One man who had temporarily lost his ability to produce testosterone found himself staring at the wall without any desire to do anything at all. Once his missing testosterone was replaced, he was once again filled with a passion for life.

This story and others like it are testimony to the fact that biology is destiny and in this case, biology can largely determine the level of your passion for life. Traders who feel no passion for their trading or anything else for that matter, may be dealing with a biological issue, rather than a psychological one. If you suspect that you are dealing with a biological issue, then you should consider a checkup with a medical professional who can test and treat you for this condition.

## IMAGINATION AND PASSION

People who lack imagination often lack passion. One of the key ingredients in passion is a vivid imagination. The sights, sounds, tastes, and all the other details of an image are the elements of passion. This is why someone who is setting the scene of a seduction brings all the elements of the senses together—the flowers, the music, the lighting, the wine, and the foods to excite the senses and a lovely room with a view and the perfect clothing and perfumes and candles.

For passion to exist where there was no passion previously, the senses must be aroused with details that make the imagination work. The awareness of these details stimulate the senses, which in turn help the brain to release the neurotransmitters that make us feel alive with passion.

The natural level of passion in a human being can be dramatically stunted by the exposure to loss, humiliation, rejection, criticism, or traumatic experiences. The images formed in the unconscious from these experiences are powerful enough to dampen the urge to feel passion for life and for the choices we make.

This area is particularly amenable to significant improvement by working with someone who is trained to help you develop a powerful set of images that can motivate you and dramatically increase your passion for trading and help to undo damaging images that decrease passion.

## A PASSION FOR HEALTH

Good health supports strong passions. Studies show that exercise not only releases neurotransmitters such as beta-endorphins and serotonin but it promotes the flow of the body's hormones. Without a heart pump to circulate its hormones, the endocrine system depends on the contraction of muscles to move its hormones around the body. So, exercise is vital to the support of passion.

But, good nutrition and rest are just as important to passion as exercise. Poor diets deplete the body of vital nutrients that produce the neurochemicals, hormones, and energy that support the feelings of passion for life.

Again, this is an area in which you can make dramatic improvements on your own or under the direction of a professional nutritionist and/or physical trainer. Even a simple gym membership that you actually use can help you to make measurable improvements in your level of passion.

## CONCLUSION

Passion is a vital part of a successful trading career. While some are born with abundant passion, the rest of us may need help in blossoming passion in our professional lives. The good news is that there are ways in which we can develop or increase our level of passion. For example, we can explore our trading for areas of latent passion or work with a professional to increase our psychological resources and our health. The first step is recognizing the need for passion; the next step is making an assessment of our current levels; and the third step is developing a plan of attack, enlisting help, and getting started.

---

*When you find it uncomfortable to not follow your rules, you have arrived as a winning trader.*

---

CHAPTER 36

# The Winner's State of Mind

Maintaining a winner's state of mind is the key to ever-expanding success in all areas of life. For a trader, it can make the difference between losing money and a high level of performance and everything in between. Here are key ingredients for reaping the rewards of successful trading.

## ENERGY

The choices you make in how you eat, drink, exercise, think, and rest will have an effect on the energy you have for your trading and your life.

### Food and Drink

These provide nutrition and therefore energy to your body—and depending upon your choices, they will either give you additional energy or take it away.

### Exercise

Exercise on a daily basis is important to keep a positive state of mind, but it is also important that you don't overdo it. You will be able to tell if you are overdoing the time or the intensity of exercise by whether you feel energized or exhausted one hour after you awaken in the morning. A general rule of thumb is at least 20 minutes to one hour of exercise per day. All exercise is not equal, depending upon repetitions, weight, and energy expended. So, adjust the time accordingly.

### Positive Thinking

Positive thinking creates a happy state of mind. When negative thinking creeps into your mind, make a list of actions that you can do and/or a commitment to change within a specific, short timeframe. If there are circumstances that are not within your control and there is no action to take, then focus on something else that makes you feel good. A special time with special people in the past is a good place to plant your focus. Our sense memories will readily recount the story, and when you add detail to that memory, it will encourage good feelings.

### Rest

It is important to rejuvenate the body, mind, and spirit by resting, which creates a high-energy state that is essential for focused trading. You can train your body to function on less sleep and convince yourself that it is all you need, but you are borrowing on your future health. You need at least seven hours of sleep and eight for very active people.

## CONFIDENCE

Being prepared boosts your level of self-confidence above all. There are several stages of being prepared in your trading career:

- Making the commitment and starting to take action
- Acquiring the necessary resources, such as money, education, and equipment
- Completing your business plan
- Trading real money because you have tested your results and you have evidence that there is a high probability of earning a profit
- Improving your results through improving yourself with coaching

Education must continuously be a part of a trader's career. The markets and world events are always changing, and while it is important to have a good trading education, winners keep up with what is happening.

Whenever you increase your knowledge about anything and expand your awareness, it will give a boost to how you feel about your self-worth.

Other stages of preparation include:

- Making good use of time: This will make the difference in whether or not you will be on a faster track to success. Everyone has high- and low-energy times in the day. High-energy time should be delegated to the time you trade. The winning state of mind is a peak performance state. In this state you are less likely to sabotage your efforts.
- Maintaining organization: This helps to keep you as a trader focused on moments of opportunity in the market. With organization, you allow the space for opportunity to flourish.
- Having supportive equipment: Using the best equipment and software optimizes your results and will give a trader less overall stress.
- Having a nourishing environment: You need people who support your effort and who boost your morale so that it is easier to maintain a winner's mindset.
- Hiring the best: Paying the best for the best keeps associates loyal and committed to maintaining a positive and productive environment.

## DISCIPLINE IS A GIFT

Ann was one of the most positive people I ever met. She was fortunate to have two loving parents who had the perfect combination of discipline, joy, and love to raise their daughter. When Ann was 18, she lost her parents in a plane crash. Ann mourned them and continued to honor them by being the best she could be at whatever she attempted to do. After several entrepreneurial endeavors, Ann came into the trading world using her discipline skills and made all the right choices. Yes, she was successful as an average good trader, but was not satisfied with average good. She was determined to be a master trader. When I coached her, I saw the only missing ingredient was that she needed to enhance her intuitive filter indicator that she did not know she had. Ann's decisions made her a master trader and also gave her a winner's mind.

## PASSION AND PURPOSE

Passion and purpose create the motivation to do the hard stuff required to attain a goal. When a trader is passionate about his trading, he is more likely to do things that he did not feel he was capable of doing, such as assuming risk, convincing others to invest in an idea or in him, and so on.

## LEAST LIKELY TO SUCCEED

Bob barely passed his classes in high school. He hated school the way the school hated him. He was a rabble-rouser who influenced other shy kids to rebel from learning and school activities. Naturally, he did not have the grades or the intention for any kind of higher education. Bob's mother was the only one who believed that her boy would eventually succeed. When she became seriously ill, Bob became a different person. His mother was the only one who believed in him, so Bob was determined to make her feel good by making better choices.

Bob used his influence skills to become a runner at the Chicago Board of Trade and that is where he discovered his passion. He knew he had to earn more money if he was going to help his mother get the best possible care. Soon, he convinced a trader to take him on as his apprentice. Bob became obsessed with being the best trader in the S&P pit and, while he never reached that goal, he was surely one of the best. Through his mother's influence, Bob became a mentor to school children, instilling in them the importance of finding purpose and passion in life.

## THE RIGHT MINDSET

How you interpret life and your experiences can make the difference between having a winner's life or a loser's life. The following attributes make for the right mindset:

- **High expectation**—preparing for all contingencies gives winners an edge because they are less likely to dwell on fear. Fear is the number one ingredient in self-sabotage.
- **Overcoming and learning from adversity**—gives you the mind muscle to handle draw-downs and changes in the markets. Winners usually enjoy the challenge of overcoming adversity because they are calculated risk takers. A winner will find and learn the lesson and enjoy it as a reward.
- **Following the high road**—makes winners enjoy the least-traveled path. Seeking revenge or willing bad things to others, even if they have done you wrong, wastes energy, time, and focus. Winners wish their

enemy the best so they can move on and make room for like-minded people.

## A HARD AND GOOD LIFE

Ali lost his parents when he was a teenager in an attack on his village. The last thing his father said to him was that forgiveness was the answer to salvation and happiness. A married couple visiting the Middle East was looking for a guide. Ali was recommended because of his ability to speak English and his friendliness to tourists. Ali's winning personality captivated the childless couple and they invited him to come for a visit to their home in America. Ali was so grateful he did whatever he could to make himself useful. The couple was so happy to have this joyful young man in their lives that they paid for his education. Eventually, Ali worked at the man's firm and became a money manager.

## FOCUS

Focus creates states of mind. Where you focus your attention day and night will have an impact on who and what you attract. You should always focus by:

- **Avoiding negative self-talk:** Repetition of the current stories that concern you in the present and negative stories of the past create stress. A winner's mind focuses mostly on the moment of now.
- **Making a plan for life, your trading, and each day:** This gives your neurological system a map to guide you to your destination and seeks out possibilities to make your way easier.
- **Choosing your words wisely:** This makes the difference between how you react to people and how they react to you. Words have power. How you speak about yourself and others says a lot about where your focus is and the outcome you will attract in life. Everyone has qualities that people can find fault with; winners focus on the good qualities and value positive interaction with others.
- **Attracting lucky situations:** This is what winners do on a regular basis while living their lives. What makes winners lucky are the choices they make, the people they associate with, the way they spend their time, and all of the other strategies, skills, and personal qualities that I have outlined in this chapter.

## A PATH TO PASSION

When Jerry was a little boy, his father bought him an elaborate erector set that he really wanted for himself. His father said to young Jerry that in order for a building to be strong it had to have a good foundation. Together they made plans for hours to construct a whole city. Jerry's father used the construction project as a metaphor for living a good life and his son took the bait. Jerry became not only a successful trader but also a respected analyst and trading teacher. His prosperity consciousness was due to:

- **Being generous:** That is, with his time, energy, and money to others and to himself, a winner enjoys the law of tithing. It is through being generous that he learns to feel he can afford to live an affluent life.
- **Networking without expectation:** A winner enjoys service to others because he is grateful for the blessings that he has received. Networking without expectation is what makes a winner at what he does and provides him with a circle of incredible colleagues.

## CONCLUSION

Winners do not necessarily possess all of the qualities and talents listed above, nor do they always make all of the right choices, but they usually possess most of these qualities and they make most of the right choices. A winner's mind produces a winner's life, which is measured not only by the money he earns, but also by the quality of the life he leads. A winner is one who has an extraordinary life and enjoys the process of creating that life.

# Extra Services: Trading On Target

For additional information, please contact us at www.tradingontarget.com.

Be sure to ask about the savings available when you seek our services, attend a seminar, or purchase one of our packages.

## SERVICES

- **Private Consulting:** Remove the barriers to each level of success in trading and all areas of your life
- **Institutional and Corporate:** Increase production and Trading ability and teamwork

## SEMINARS

- **Top Performance:** For discipline and overcoming sabotage
- **The Winner's Edge**: Gain the technical and psychological tools for becoming a successful investor
- **Intuition/Discretionary:** Develop and use reliable intuitive indicators
- **Building a Capital and Client Base:** Build sales and increase production
- **Creating Affluence:** Increase resources and balance your life
- **Enriching Life Seminar:** Build success by making better choices and gain control over your life

## PRODUCTS

### Traders' Secrets Package #1

- *Traders' Secrets* book
- Evaluation and consultation by phone
- *Stress Relief* (2-CD album)
- One-year subscription to TOT newsletter

### Discipline Package #2

- *The Winning Edge 2* book
- *Discipline 2* (2-CD album)
- *Get a Life* book

### Winning Edge Package #3

- *The Winning Edge 1* book
- *Discipline 1* DVD
- *Six Steps to Greater Success* DVD

### Business Plan Package #4

- *The Winning Edge 3* book
- *Trader's Business Plan* book
- *Trader's Business Plan* DVD
- One-year subscription to TOT newsletter

### Interview Package #5

- *Trading on Target 3* interviews (4-CD Album)
- *Trading on Target 4* interviews (4-CD Album)
- *Dear Coach* book

### Motivational Package #6

- *The Winning Edge 4* book
- *Discipline 3* (2-CD album)
- E-Books 1 & 2 (emailed)
- One-year subscription to TOT newsletter

# Index